MIGHTY MOUSE

# MIGHTY MOUSE

## An Autobiography

## Ian McLauchlan

### with Ian Archer

**STANLEY PAUL**

London Melbourne Sydney Auckland Johannesburg

To Eileen, Andrew, Scott
and Ross

Stanley Paul & Co. Ltd

An imprint of the Hutchinson Publishing Group

3 Fitzroy Square, London w1p 6jd

Hutchinson Group (Australia) Pty Ltd
30-32 Cremorne Street, Richmond South, Victoria 3121
PO Box 151, Broadway, New South Wales 2007

Hutchinson Group (NZ) Ltd
32-34 View Road, PO Box 40-086, Glenfield, Auckland 10

Hutchinson Group (SA) (Pty) Ltd
PO Box 337, Bergvlei 2012, South Africa

First Published 1980

© Ian McLauchlan 1980

Set in VIP Baskerville by
A-Line Services, Saffron Walden, Essex

Printed in Great Britain by The Anchor Press Ltd,
and bound by Wm Brendon & Son Ltd,
both of Tiptree, Essex

British Library Cataloguing in Publication Data

McLauchlan, Ian
  Mighty Mouse.
  1. McLauchlan, Ian
  2. Rugby football players – Scotland –
  Biography
  I. Title
  796.33'3'0924    GV944.9.M3/

ISBN 0 09 143390 8

Copyright photographs are acknowledged as follows:
Sport and General Press Agency Ltd; *Die Burger*; Willie Stassen;
Perskor-Biblioteek; the *Glasgow Herald*; the (Glasgow) *Daily Record*;
the *Scotsman* Publications; John Rubython;
E. Labuschagne; Colorsport

# Contents

*To Eileen and the boys*

# I

# That Day in Dunedin

Tackle, tackle, tackle. Knock them down, knock them down, knock them down. Tackle Colin Meads, knock down Sid Going. And get up and keep running. Tackle Peter Whiting, knock down Bob Burgess. And try not to think of the minutes to the final whistle. Tackle some more, knock down anything in sight. And forget how tired you are. It'll soon be over. Try not to think of a shower or a drink. Just keep going. Just keep praying that the referee will blow the final whistle.

I've waited years for this moment and I'm damned if I'll let it slip. I'll tackle, I'll knock them down. While there's an ounce of energy left I'll use it. But when will he blow the whistle? It's agony. We've won. We haven't won. Not yet anyway. Barry John's penalty a couple of minutes ago must have settled it. That put us 9–3 ahead and we can't get beaten now. Don't think like that. Keep tackling. Think rugby, keep moving. Sean's puffing and blowing, I know how he feels. But don't let New Zealand see how tired we are. They're the same, they must be after a match like this.

Barry looks as concerned as a man doing the crossword puzzle, contented, even amused. He's won the match for us. I've done my bit, more than my bit but don't count the glory just yet. That will come later. It'll last for years. Don't think of Eileen. Think about the next scrum. Hope it's the last. They call this enjoying yourself. That's bloody right. What's the word for someone who loves pain? Masochist, that's it.

He's blown the final whistle. I don't believe it. We've won. We've won. New Zealand 3; British Lions 9. Throw your hands in the air, hug the nearest man to you. Commiserate with the All Blacks. Some players, they are. Get into the

7

dressing room. It's all over. We've won. We've bloody well won.

The British Lions had come to New Zealand in 1971, not so much as a rugby squad, more a group of sacrificial lambs ready to be slaughtered by the All Blacks. I had arrived a little bit wet behind the ears, honoured to be included, not really expecting to play in any Tests. It had stayed that way until a week before the match against New Zealand at Dunedin. Then Ray McLoughlin was hurt in a brawl at Canterbury. Suddenly I was first choice.

That Test changed my life. Before it I was Ian McLauchlan (Jordanhill and Scotland), who had taken an awful long time to persuade selectors that he wasn't too small to play for his country. Afterwards – when the Lions manager Doug Smith coined the phrase – I was Mighty Mouse. But I didn't know that the day we were in the bus going from the airport into Dunedin and they read out the team for the match. J.P.R. Williams, John Bevan, John Dawes (captain), Mike Gibson, Gerald Davies, Barry John, Gareth Edwards . . . then Ian McLauchlan.

On the Friday night Willie John McBride invited the forwards to his room in the Southern Cross Hotel. The atmosphere was sombre. We seemed an awful long long way from home. Clearly – and picking his words with care – Willie John started talking to us. To me and John Pullin and Sean Lynch, to Delme Thomas and John Taylor, to Peter Dixon and Mervyn Davies. There was no wild talk.

'A lot you will think you have been in hard matches and possibly you have. But wait until tomorrow. It will be the hardest game of your lives. The All Blacks will hit us with everything except the kitchen sink. Maybe they will hit us with that as well.'

'They've got to beat us. There's a whole country here which is telling them they've got to beat us. They will be out to give us a doing. Think about it. Then go to bed and have a good night's sleep.' I slept. I've never had any trouble with nerves that way.

In the morning I got up about nine o'clock. I had the usual McLauchlan breakfast . . . cornflakes, bacon and eggs, toast, tea. It would take more than a First Test Match to ruin my appetite. I watched the television and I mooched about a bit. Carwyn James, the coach, asked to see us for a team talk. Quietly, just like Willie John, he gave the Lions his expert advice. We listened.

He told us to scrummage well. He told us when and where to wheel that scrummage. But again, it was downbeat, deliberately low key so that we would not go and play the Test Match there and then. That would have to wait until we arrived at Carisbrook, and the referee John Pring blew his whistle for the kick off and 45,000 New Zealanders started baying for our blood. In the meantime, it was a case of 'Remember this; don't forget that.'

John Dawes, the captain, spoke and was quick and to the point: 'It will be hard. If we don't match them, they will trample all over us. But we know we are the better team.' He turned to the forwards: 'Just give us the ball,' he said.

We left the dressing room and ran on to the pitch. The place was absolutely packed and there wasn't even a gap in the 'Scotsman's' stand, the railway embankment at Carisbrook where thousands could get a free view of the match. Before I knew it we were playing.

The first man I saw was the All Black prop, Jazz Muller, the eighteen-and-a-half stone guy who was my immediate opponent. 'Christ!' I thought to myself. 'I've got to hump that about all afternoon.' But there wasn't much time for philosophy.

The first fifteen minutes were the hardest rugby I have ever played – before or since. I wasn't nervous. I had trained and prepared for this moment for months, even years. They kept coming at us, again and again. We won most of the scrummages, gave the ball to Barry John and he kicked and kept us in the match. I wasn't nervous. The fact that it was physical didn't bother me. The only anxiety was born out of a desperation to succeed. It was murder because they looked so much stronger, so much bigger, so much faster and so much fitter than we were. Despite all the pre-match pep talks we were still a bit in awe of them. We had all played them back in Britain . . . and not beaten them. And here we were, on their own cabbage patch, and here were Messrs Meads, Whiting, Kirkpatrick, three of the most feared players in the world. They were superb.

But slowly they began to make mistakes. Barry had this marvellous knack of just kicking to where fullback Fergie McCormack or the covering wing were not. That gave us a lift. Let's play for Barry, we all thought.

Jazz wasn't giving me any trouble. I burrowed in underneath him. John Pullin was staying very cool, winning the ball every time Gareth put it in. Sean Lynch was muttering 'Be Jesus', which meant he was enjoying it. We knew we had them worried when they started throwing punches early on but we gave as good as we got. That settled the dust and we were determined to win the match.

Then Gareth pulled his hamstring. That was a downer but Chico Hopkins came on and we never noticed the difference. He made some cheeky little breaks. The All Blacks were now making quite a few mistakes but it wasn't getting any easier.

Just before half-time we won the ball on the right. John Bevan crashed through the middle but the ball was dislodged from his hand. One of our lads kicked through. I was running down the middle of the field in support as the All Blacks, under a bit of pressure, tried to tidy up. Sid Going passed back to Alan Sutherland, behind his own line. All I could think of was getting to Sutherland and in the process barged down Fergie McCormack. Sutherland prepared to kick as I closed in. I put my hands up to block the ball and felt leather hit my forearm. I saw it straight away. Obligingly, it had nestled a couple of yards from me and over the All Black line. I just had to drop on it. Easy. Unbelievably, there was no one around. You could have heard a pin drop. 'It can't be a try,' I thought. 'It must be a knock on.' But the referee had already blown his whistle. It was a try. Then I permitted myself a little smile. Inwardly, I was beaming. I didn't believe it was happening. We were in the lead, I had scored against the All Blacks in their own country. It was only hours later that it dawned on me what it all meant. Meanwhile there was still a game to be played.

And we won it. Fergie McCormack brought the All Blacks

level, but Barry kicked a couple of penalties and so the game went on and on.

Tackle, tackle tackle. Knock them down, knock them down, knock them down. And blow that bloody whistle. At last he did, the sweetest sound in the world. In the tunnel Doug Smith was waiting. 'You', he said, and it was the first time anyone had ever used the phrase, 'are some Mighty Mouse.'

# 2

# The First Lesson

I didn't know what rugby was until I was twelve. In Tarbolton, the little mining village in Ayrshire where I was born and raised, sport meant football, racing pigeons, whippets, pitch-and-toss . . . and more football. I doubt if anyone in the place had any idea where Murrayfield was, let alone been there.

Home was a big detached house in Croft Street. Father was a miner, a tough gentle guy who could usually be found most nights sitting by the fire reading a Sir Walter Scott novel. Mother could be found in the kitchen, doting on her children, myself and sisters Grace, Ellen and Kay.

The garden was enormous. As soon as I could walk, Dad would take his nose out of his book and have me out there kicking a ball about. A round one, of course. He had been a useful player in his time, turning out for Ardrossan Winton Rovers in Ayrshire Junior football, the sort of stuff which at times could make a Test Match against the All Blacks look like a vicarage tea party. If you think that is an exaggeration, ask Bill Shankly who came from down the road with Glenbuck Cherrypickers. It wasn't unknown for players to come straight from the pit, pull a jersey over their shoulders and play in their boots.

Everyone played football. It was the great activity which bound the community together. As soon as you got home from school, you couldn't wait to get out with a ball. That was how it was all the time I was at primary school: except for the first two days, when I didn't even bother to wait for school to finish. I took one look at the place, ran straight home at nine o'clock in the morning and started practising my 'keepie uppies' on the lawn. Mother was distinctly unamused.

I did well enough at primary school. They gave me a medal for winning the obstacle race at the Coronation Sports. Mother thought I had won the mile as well when she turned up a little bit late. She didn't realize that I was a lap behind. I've never been the greatest speed merchant.

When I was eleven, I left the primary school and went to Ayr Academy. Ayr's about seven miles away from Tarbolton and it seemed like a huge metropolis, the centre of the universe at the time. Three or four other lads from the village won places, but an awful lot didn't and as we set off on the bus, kitted out in our maroon blazers, some of the others looked upon us as 'Snobby Joes.'

They thought we had made a big social step away from them. And a lot wanted nothing to do with us at all. When we came back in the evening – dropping the satchel at the house – we headed for the park and a game of football. They would be waiting for us, determined to get their own back. There wasn't one thing they would stop at inside or outside the rules. Hacking, tripping, you name it, they knew it and they would dish it out.

There was only one reply – to dish it out back. It taught me a lesson which has proved invaluable in places like Cardiff and Capetown. Don't nurse greivances, just sort the thing out there and then. That way you don't just stop it from going on. You win some respect as well. These football matches hardened my character.

It was my eldest sister Grace, who was a tennis player of no mean ability, who gave me some important advice when I went to the Academy: 'You're nothing there unless you are good at sport. Especially rugby. So get stuck into it.' Luckily I came under the influence of a remarkable man and never looked back.

T.B. Watson, the PE teacher at Ayr Academy, was a man from another world. He'd lived most of his life in the army and although he was now in civvie street, his department was run like the forces. He did everything by numbers. 'I want my boys clean and tidy, hard and strong,' he would say. He was a fairly awesome character.

So, too was the Rector of the Academy, J.D. Cairns, and

one of his hobbies was coaching the second-year rugby side. He was a man of about sixty then and used to turn up at the practices wearing his pin-striped suit and spectacles. But that didn't stop him from joining in.

There was hardly any way that you could avoid rugby at the Academy. Most PE lessons concentrated on rugby in the gym, passing, tackling, learning the basic skills. Once a week, we went to the school playing fields at the Old Racecourse and it was there I played my first ever game . . . in the second row. I knew right away this was the game for me and Tuesday afternoons became the best part of the school curriculum. Within weeks, I was playing against other local schools in the first year's top team. I was never dropped, not throughout my schooldays or by a club.

We were very successful too, hardly losing a match. In fact we became so blasé that the Rector arrived during the second year for one of our sessions and decided we needed a gee-up. He became rather agitated about the tackling . . . or lack of it. So off came the pin-striped jacket and the glasses and he thundered at us: 'Just run at me. I'll stop you.' And we all went down one by one. We didn't miss any tackles after that, not in practice or a team game.

The Rector liked me. I was only in trouble once. In fourth year we'd been giving the teacher some mayhem, sitting with our feet on desks. She took me out in front of the class and gave me six with the belt. As far as the pain was concerned she might have been hitting me with a cushion. So she sent me to see the Rector which was the last straw or the only option available, depending on your point of view.

J.D. gave me four more of the belt which, as far as any physical reprimand was concerned, was another useless exercise. Then he looked at me and said, 'McLauchlan, I expected more from you.' It was the only time in my life that I've felt completely embarrassed and upset. There was an odd sequel. When I got home I discovered that another Tarbolton boy had told my father, who gave me a dressing down. But dad inadvertently let slip the name of the guy who had 'cliped' on me. I was straight out of the house afterwards and gave him a real doing. And I mean a real doing.

My other mentor, T.B., got me involved in other sports, notably boxing. He was very keen on it and at the end of every February there were the annual school championships, a big event in the life of the school. They were always held in the main hall right in the middle of the school and a sell-out was guaranteed. T.B. loved it. 'Come over here lad,' he would say; 'You look like a light middleweight.' And he would hand the guy a pair of gloves and tell him to get on with it. You weren't permitted to be a coward.

I boxed for six years and had about twenty fights before I retired undefeated. I may not have been a Muhammad Ali but at least I had the sense to quit while I was ahead. My style was that of a classical brawler. The other guy might outjab me and outpoint me but I just waded in and tried to put him away. It seemed to work. 'They can run but they can't hide,' as Ali said. The boxing wasn't just confined to school. I went to the local YMCA and sparred and fought there. But when I was seventeen I decided the time had come to quit. Sometime soon I would be up against a guy who could punch as well as box . . . and I didn't fancy the thought of taking a hammering.

Summers were a bit of a bore. I had a go at cricket but never seemed to get to the crease. The trouble was that there was a fellow called Mike Denness in the same side and he batted all afternoon most times. I tried athletics – 800 metres was my distance – but never got very interested. On holiday I would work for thirty bob a day on a farm just outside Tarbolton which helped to keep me fit. But even then, the most important dates on the calendar were around the end of August when the rugby began again.

By the age of fourteen the game had become the be-all and end-all of my life. I trained twice a week at school and would go out running in the evening with the family dogs, Major and Tiki, over the fields around Tarbolton. By the time I was in my fourth year at the Academy, I was in the First XV, one of the two youngest members of the side. Denness, who would have played for Scotland at rugby if he hadn't concentrated on that other game, was the centre. The fly-half was another lad who would have made it had he stuck to rugby. Instead Ian Ure went off to play for Manchester United and Arsenal.

The Academy took the game seriously and winning was important. But there was time for plenty of fun. In the third year we were coached by Bill Beckles, the school's modern language teacher, who one day decided to stand on his head in the middle of the pitch during a practice: 'Sorry boys, it doesn't look like rugby from this angle either,' he said. We played basic running rugby which is all I would advocate for any kid of that age. The theory and the tactics can come later. The most important things is to have everyone involved for as much time as possible.

I don't suppose that between my second and sixth year at the Academy I played on a losing side more than half-a-dozen times. That's how good we were. And we were competing against all the schools in the West of Scotland.

Life was good, a steady round of sport and, in between times, just enough studying to get by. I ended up with five highers – English, Geography, Maths, Science and Technical Studies. That was enough to get me into University had I wanted to go.

Dad had vague ambitions that I should be a doctor. Like a lot of miners, he didn't want me to have anything to do with the pits and education was the way out. But he realized that it was a losing battle as far as I was concerned because my mind had been made up for quite a long time that I wanted to play games and be a teacher. Jordanhill College – the PE college for Scotland – was the place for me. When I was in the sixth year, I presented myself there and was accepted. Dad was a trifle upset, but he knew he had been fighting a losing battle.

Already I had received some recognition outside of Ayr. In my fifth year I had been chosen to play for Glasgow Schools against Edinburgh. The next season I played a complete set of games and it was on the way back from Gala where we had been playing the South Schools that I learned another invaluable lesson for any rugby player – how to handle the drink.

Some of the lads from the big city schools – Glasgow Academy, Hutchesons, High School – produced the 'carry out'. The teachers were in the next compartment, having a noggin of their own and generally keeping out of the way. So we dived into the booze, whisky, vodka, beer, the lot. I've no idea how I got back to Tarbolton that night. Half the side were being sick all over the place. To tell you the truth I didn't like the stuff all that much then, although I've come to appreciate it now. Just a little.

I've never touched a drop on the evening before a match although there have been times when I've seen a few Scottish teammates so nervous on the eve of an international that a few pints might have been the best medicine for them.

I went to Jordanhill in 1960 to read a three-year Diploma Course in physical education. I felt right at home straight away because more than half the course was practical and I could try my hand at no end of sports I'd never played – volleyball, basketball and hockey for example. They made me goalkeeper at the hockey because not only did I cover most of the goal but any time an attacker entered the circle I could have a kick at him. It was the fittest I've ever been in my life before or since.

Within days, I'd met this funny little guy with specs who was to become the major influence on my sporting life – Bill Dickinson, a lecturer at college and the man in charge of rugby. He took the first practice and the boy up from the country was eager to impress. I had by this time been shuttled from the second row to wing forward and hared about all over the college grounds. Afterwards he came up to me and said, 'Look son. You're not fast enough to play in the back row and you're not strong enough to play in the front.' You could imagine what that did to the confidence of Ian McLauchlan, big hero at Ayr Academy, just waiting to take the world by storm. The little man added, 'Not at this level, anyway.' He meant club rugby and I thought that it was a terrible insult.

It was my first meeting with this extraordinary man and what I have achieved with Jordanhill and Scotland has been largely due to him. Bill has lived, eaten and probably slept rugby since the end of the War. He was the man who brought respectability to coaching in this country. He's my big mentor really.

I got over this first exchange and started working hard to

gain my place in the College side. 'I'll show him' was my attitude. At that time I was 11 stone 4 lbs and I realized that I had to build myself up if there was to be a rugby future. At nights I would go back to the college gym for weight training and three months later I was 13 stone 10 lbs and Dickie was having to look at me in a new light.

By New Year, he gave me a game at prop in the Second XV, the first time I had ever played in the position. We played Aberdeen Grammar FP and I scored three tries. A week later I was in the big team which travelled to Langholm, which was a baptism by fire for any eighteen-year-old.

Jock Beattie, the Hawick worthy, once said of Langholm in a pep talk to his team: 'Remember lads, there are thousands of them.' That's how it's seemed to me down the years. They may not have the best team in the Borders, but they play a fervent brand of rugby and you sometimes stop and start counting how many red jerseys there are on the field. They also have a great 'rent-a-crowd'. There might only be 200 supporters but they run up and down the touchline with the play, generally bawling and shouting at you.

This was where it all started.

It was one of those wet dark dank days. There was mud, blood and snotters all over the pitch. Before the game, Dickie pulled me aside for a wee chat. 'This is what you do. You hold up your side of the scrum. At line-outs you block and make sure nothing passes you. If you happen to get the ball in your hands, go straight forward and knock someone down. If you are in a situation where someone has the ball in *his* hands and is coming straight at you, knock *him* down. And I mean *down – dead*. And by the way, don't do anything else. Come to think of it, you won't be good enough to do anything else.'

I went out and followed his instructions to the letter of the law. I had my hands on the ball just twice. I knocked people down and laid the ball back. I left quite a few guys for dead. What I remember most is the Langholm prop, whoever he might have been, going down in one scrum, picking up a clump of mud and shoving it straight down my mouth. I was too busy spitting out the mud to do anything about it but it's not a bad trick really. It does tend to keep people quiet.

We lost. But I felt I had done all right and so did my teammates. Dickie, cautious as ever, contented himself with the observation, 'There's a bit of work to do yet.' But I was on my way.

# 3

# A Man's Game

I'm a very violent person really. You won't find many guys in the middle of an international scrum who are the sort of fellows likely to turn the other cheek. You have to learn to look after yourself one way or another – otherwise you're dead. One day we were coming back on the train from Murrayfield to Glasgow, a carriage load of rugby men, hard cases all.

Talk turned to the nasties, to the worst punch-ups and incidents we had ever seen on the field.

There were the usual stories of people being trampled on in the rucks, of studs being scraped across their faces, of ears being bitten. Now I've never consciously done anything like that. In twenty years, I've never been sent off... and it wasn't until 1973 that I ever played in a game where anyone *was* dismissed. I've been hard and looked after myself. But I was certain that I had never been dirty.

Mike Hunter, a teammate in the Glasgow side, took up the conversation. 'I was playing for Glasgow High one day. And was making a run. Suddenly I was flattened by a stiff-arm tackle. Right round the head. It needed twenty-two stitches in the mouth after that one. Definitely the worst thing that ever happened to me'.

'Who were you playing?' I asked.

'Jordanhill, your team', he replied.

'And who did it to you.'

'You did, you bugger.'

That stopped me in my tracks. I searched about trying to remember the match, remember the moment. I just about managed to recall a game about three years before when I'd tackled Mike. Yet all that came back was not the tackle, just standing over him and thinking to myself, 'Good, they're down to fourteen men.' I never thought twice about it afterwards. I just wanted to make that tackle like I've made thousands of others.

I'm not a hypocrite. Rugby is a game which can always be violent and I've been the sort of player who has never run away from a fight. I've fought with some of my best pals in the game. Once, I left-hooked Micky Burton during an England match at Murrayfield, right in front of the Queen, who was a spectator that day. Micky said to me afterwards: 'It wasn't the punch which worried me. It was the fact that you did it in front of Her Majesty.' Maybe I would have been sent to the Tower of London if she understood the rules of the game.

In fact there are two sets of rules: those which are official and those which are unwritten. All top players know them and respect opponents who play by them. I wouldn't have played forty-three times for Scotland and gone on two British Lions tours if I were the sort of person who couldn't look after himself. But it's important to understand the ways in which an international player can mess about – and the acts which fall totally outside the spirit of the game.

In recent years rugby has been under a cloud because of dirty play – and television close-ups and action-replays have all helped to damage the game's image amongst people who don't understand it. When I watched New Zealander John Ashworth raking his studs across J. P. R. Williams' head I was as horrified as the next man because it simply isn't the way the game should be played, no matter what had gone on before.

There are things you can do in rugby and things which you can't and shouldn't do. Kicking an opponent is out under any circumstances and so is the intentional straight-arm tackle. They fall outside the code of honour and I would support any referee who sent a player off for such fouls, and back any rugby union which banned the player for life. The game doesn't need people like that. Indeed it can't afford them.

The growth of rugby in my time has been dependent upon persuading parents that it's the best game in the world for their children and that kind of incident must make them wonder whether it's a bloodsport rather than just a game. Three times, refereeing schoolboy matches, I have sent youngsters off, once for swearing, twice for punching. Kids can be bullied on a rugby pitch and that has to be stamped out right away.

But for adults, it's a man's game, rightly so. I'm a member of an international brotherhood known as the Front Row Union. Or as some like to say 'The Mafia'. And over the years we have worked out our own code of honour.

My job as a loose head prop is to protect my hooker and help win the ball. If I fall down in that task, every other member of the team is going to struggle on starvation rations and not enjoy the game. And I simply won't allow myself to be defected from that task.

So the messing about starts. Your opponent will try and pull you down; he will bore in on the hooker or grab your jersey. That leaves you with a difficult decision, whether to accept that or do something about it – in short, nip it in the bud straight away. I've always worked on the principle of giving him a sharp reminder that we are not going to play the game that way, and that's often involved a short left hook to the jaw.

Most times he will get the message and we settle down to play rugby. Which is the object of the exercise anyway. Quite often referees will almost be grateful that the pair of you have established the ground rules without bothering him. And despite the fact that it can get rough, ther's usually a lot of honour in the front row. I like the story of two Scottish players – Struan McCallum of Jordanhill and Jock Craig of Ayr – who were battling it out at Millbrae one afternoon. The referee said to them, 'If you two want to box, then get behind the stand and do it.' Struan replied: 'You can't do that, ref, the crowd will go with us.'

The Mafia's rules are quite strict. For example, we don't go messing about with threequarters, because they are the *prima donnas* of the game – although some of them wouldn't make bad members of the Front Row Union themselves. It would be a brave man who took on J.P.R. Williams, Steve Fenwick or Alistair Cranston.

In many ways it's a question of survival, particularly at international level. When we went to New Zealand as British Lions we knew that if we didn't look after ourselves, then there wouldn't have been a contest. The All Blacks would have walked all over us. And it was the same in South Africa – even more so – three years later.

So those tours were at times violent. But at that level, the experienced player has a cut-off point. Inevitably, because you are playing for the highest stakes of your life, there are moments when the tempers flair. But they were never really vicious. I did a lot of sorting out – with help from my friends – but there was no occasion on which I went mental. I had self-control all the time.

It's simply this. To gain the respect of your fellow-players, you've got to establish a reputation as a man who will stand his ground when the going gets tough. That applies at club and international level. On the other hand, anyone who oversteps the mark between messing about and acting like a psychopath won't be tolerated either, because he's a menace to the rest of us – and the game in general.

I'm a hard man who's played in a hard school. I like the saying they have in the Borders at Langholm when the referee is threatening to send someone off: 'Leave him on ref,' they will plead. That is a fate worse than death.

I have brawled with the best of them all round the world but I can go to bed at night and sleep easy knowing that I have never deliberately injured anyone, never overstepped the unwritten rules of our game and never had an occasion on which someone wouldn't buy me a drink after a match. That's the best part of rugby: having a pint and comparing notes on how far your right hook travelled, and wondering which of you will have the bigger and better bruises the next morning. Mostly, it was the other guy.

# 4

# Home Rule in Scotland

It's a crying shame that Bill Dickinson never managed or coached a British Lions side. He made Jordanhill a club which was respected rather than ignored by the Old School tie set who didn't want Scottish Rugby to change. They were happy with the closed shop of traditional fixtures and wanted that cosy set-up to carry on forever. When he coached the national side he transformed it into a team which every other country feared – and hardly even raised his voice in doing so.

I'd only been in the Jordanhill side half a season when I nearly got dropped for the first and only time. It happened after the single run-in I ever had with the man. We were on a tour to Workington, Carlisle and Jedforest and the young McLauchlan was anxious to prove that he had come of age. On the field it was no problem. I was learning all the time and I was getting stronger. Off the field it was more difficult.

The tour progressed in a sea of pints and gin-and-tonics with the old lags leading me on. 'Have another one, Ian!' was the cry. I didn't like to let the team down. By the time we reached the Borders there wasn't much blood in the alcohol system and I wasn't getting too much sensation from my legs. We were holding out 8–6 against Jed when they dropped a goal; we lost, and we thought that was that.

Back in the dressing room – just for once – Dickie blew a gasket. Or rather several gaskets. He was absolutely furious, took the whole side apart and said that none of us would ever play for the club again unless we straightened ourselves out. It was another salutory lesson early in my career and I took it to heart. I wasn't in fact dropped but I had discovered the attitude which was to take the club and myself to the very top of Scottish rugby.

Dickie had two great disadvantages. He wasn't from an 'established' club and he had never played international rugby. Some people who don't know anything about the game still hold that against him. There were people in Scottish rugby always trying to discredit him, and Jordanhill. Some clubs simply didn't want to play us because we were upstarts and they would invent stories that we were butchers. Funny that this always happened just after we had beaten them.

Jordanhill was a small club – and not very fashionable at all. Yet it won the unofficial Scottish Championship in 1968 and that was due to Dickie's coaching as much as anything. That year we beat Hawick and we beat Langholm, largely because we were clear in every game just exactly what we were trying to achieve. Dickie's philosophy was very easy to understand. We had a super pack and were determined to put that to good use. Yet all that led to was criticism about Jordanhill playing dour ten-man rugby.

All I can say is that Jordanhill had its best period when he was in charge and so had Scotland when he was adviser to the national side. I want to explode this myth of ten-man rugby here and now. The myth states that the forwards and half-backs do all the work while the backs hang around picking their noses, wondering when the bar opens and thinking about what disco they will go to that night. Nothing could be further from the truth.

There isn't such a game as ten-man rugby. Dickie always insisted that the backs had a role to play. The forwards were the platform. If any back got into trouble, he was told to seek out forwards, cut in towards them, let them re-win the ball and set up another attacking movement. The emphasis was always on attack and I'll bet that Jordanhill's threequarters scored more points than most over the course of a season.

Certainly, there were muddy, rainy days when we hugged the touchline and used the power of our forwards, but there were days when Hawick and Gala did the same. We were always prepared to run the ball when it was sensible to do so. I put down all the criticism we took at that time to that old

Scottish trait of knocking winners. We build up our heroes and then we can't wait to push them off that pedestal.

The New Zealanders played the same system for many, many years; they came across to Britain and wiped the floor with the four home countries and there wasn't much said about their tactics being wrong. The only trouble was that Jordanhill was interfering with the natural order of things in Scottish rugby and people were being forced to sit up and take notice.

It's one thing to know how you want to play, and something else entirely to make it actually happen. That was Dickie's other secret. He took a great many players who had no natural rugby pedigree and made them into good players. Myself included. Struan McCallum was another. He had never played the game at all until second year at College, yet he went on to captain the Scotland 'B' side for two years.

Dickie was a great amateur psychologist as well. A side is made up of fifteen separate people who have to be welded into a unit and he realized the important point that individuals all needed different handling. Over the years, he kept me in check.

One season I had been playing for the Glasgow District side most midweeks. As we sat in the dressing room one Saturday, he turned to me and asked: 'Who do you play for?' 'Jordanhill,' I replied. 'No you don't. You play for Glasgow and you only go through the motions for the club. This is your last chance. Either you play well today, or you're out.'

Another guy was once stupid enough to say that he could get a game for the West of Scotland, our deadliest local rivals. Dickie reached into his pocket and brought out a ten bob note which he gave to the player. 'There you are, that'll cover your bus fares for the month. When you need some more money just come back and I'll give it to you.'

A couple of years after I made my debut at Langholm, we went back there and won a really hard match. I received a warning for over-robust play: I'd broken my nose and I limped off the pitch totally exhausted. Our victory had been gained by the Jordanhill wing threequarter Peter Connelly, one of those people who was always liable to run in two or three tries for you but who wasn't always around when the bugle really sounded. Peter came off, a match-winner without a drop of mud on his jersey.

I thought he was bound to get a rollicking despite the fact that he had won the game for us. But when we did get into the dressing room, Dickie went up to him and said 'Oh, Peter son, what would we do without you.' That surprised me a bit but I just thought that Bill was in a good mood and it was to be a case of handing out the praise all round. So I sat there, vaguely worried about the shape of my nose and what it would do to my chances of getting a date that night, and waited for the laurel wreaths to be passed in my direction.

'As for you McLauchlan, you missed a tackle out there,' he said. And just turned away from me. I was cursing but I never missed another tackle that season. He knew how to deflate me. But he knew that a rebuke would also make me more determined.


I'd been twelve years a rugby player; I'd played against Wales, England, Ireland, Argentina, Australia and New Zealand and South Africa. Yet I'd never played against Heriots, Edinburgh's top club, or against Melrose, one of the strongest Border teams. Jordanhill couldn't get a fixture against either of them. That was a crazy way to run the game in Scotland.

Then in 1973, the Scottish Rugby Union decided to introduce the Leagues. That surprised many people who thought that the Union had only just caught on to the fact that Queen Victoria was dead.

Before that there had been the unofficial Championship, really a press invention, and it was based on percentage points. We were delighted to win it in 1968 but it wasn't the real thing simply because you didn't play every other side in the table. Our fixture list included games against all the other Glasgow clubs, but not Heriots, not Melrose and Gala wouldn't play us on a Saturday.

The League changed all that overnight. Jordanhill were automatically placed in the First Division because of their record over the previous years – and smaller clubs across the country like Preston Lodge, Clarkston, Highland and Haddington all had very good reason to improve themselves, because there was nothing to stop them going all the way to the top.

If there was ever a man who proved the success of the Leagues it was Nairn McEwan. Nairn had decided that if he wanted to get into the Scottish side, he would have to leave the Inverness club Highland and go elsewhere. He chose Gala, the only Borders team which draws its players from all airts and pairts. Having achieved his ambition – and with the Leagues in operation – he felt he could go back to his local side and still continue to receive international recognition. That saved him a 400-mile round trip at weekends and he carried Highland into the First Division. His story proves that the Leagues were an instant success.

There are still a few committee men about today who believe that the SRU acted like revolutionaries, that they were so far out of character that what they had done was about as surprising as Margaret Thatcher joining the Communist Party. But that number is decreasing every year and the diehards brought up on Former Pupils Rugby and a sociable fixture list are becoming a breed as extinct as dinosaurs.

The League made all the difference to Jordanhill. Immediately the game became more intense. Our club had always taken the game very seriously – with Dickie there was no alternative – and we soon found representatives from other clubs turning up and asking for information, while coaches were appearing just to watch our training sessions. We, in turn, always made it a point to ensure that one or two committee men would go and see the team we were due to play the following Saturday. Training generally had a sharper edge.

That was basically what the players wanted. I know there is a body of opinion which sees rugby as the last bastion of the beer-swilling executive who just wants a run out every Saturday afternoon. And I'd be the last man to deny him that right. There are plenty of places in the Third XVs for them to have a convivial day out. Especially if he wants to buy me a few beers afterwards. But once players have competed at the top level, they are only interested in gaining a standard of excellence in a sport which has become their way of life – and for which they have sacrificed a lot in terms of family life. The Leagues were invented to help that kind of player and the sort of clubs which would encourage him.

The great worry among some SRU members was that League rugby would be a dirtier game. It was understandable to an extent. Rugby men watch other sports and they feared that some of the nastier kinds of professionalism which have crept into soccer would rub off on our game as well. Those fears were unfounded.

But the SRU did make a mistake at that time by instructing referees to clamp down on dirty play. At first sight, fair enough. But the message was taken too literally by some referees in the lower divisions and the result was a massive increase in the numbers of orderings-off. It led to some hysterical publicity and a poor image for the game. Reports didn't tally with what actually happened on the pitch, at least not in the First Division. In all my time at Jordanhill, I have only ever played in two matches where players were sent off, and for anyone who thinks the Leagues have led to mayhem it's interesting to describe what happened on each occasion.

The first was a right old laugh. We were playing Gala and Hugh McPherson, our wing forward, was sent off with just ten seconds of the game remaining. In fact, Arthur Brown kicked the penalty which followed straight into touch and referee Eddie Sherritt then blew the whistle for no-side. When we asked Eddie why he had sent Hugh off, he claimed that he had taken someone out of the ruck a bit hard. The joke was that the referee went up to another of our players afterwards – Hugh Campbell – and asked for his name and address to send to the SRU. It was a classic case of mistaken identity. That left Campbell in an awkward situation. If he had volunteered his own name, the whole matter would have been laughed out of court but the problem was that he had a 'B' international coming up the next week and didn't want to take the rap. So poor Hugh McPherson was suspended for a month.

The second was, in its own way, just as hilarious – and it concerned the best referee in the country, Alan Hosie. Jordanhill were playing Edinburgh Wanderers and one of their forwards stamped on our scrum-half Robin Ford. The mistake this guy made was that he was spotted doing it by our second row man Wes Wyroslawski, a guy who tends not to need any encouragement on these occasions. Wes took off after the Wanderers man and it's fair to say that he wasn't approaching him just to enquire about the time of day. Alan's a good referee and he knew that if Wes caught up with his man, then the next call would be 999 for an ambulance. So he blows the whistle while Wes is still five yards away from his prey and sends him off. Strictly speaking a correct decision, but what followed wasn't. He was suspended for six weeks.

I could name you one guy in Scottish rugby who's been sent off three times and his top suspension has been four weeks. Every case has to be assessed on its merits – if that's the right word! – but surely the more often you get into trouble, the more severe the penalties should be.

So dirty play – in my experience – has not been brought about because of the coming of the Leagues. Possibly the reverse. What use is a player to his club if he is suspended and they have a promotion or relegation fight on their hands. Teammates and club officials can exert as much authority over the culprits as can the SRU by reminding them of their responsibilities, forcibly if need be.

That's not to say that everything is right with the Leagues. Or with Scottish rugby generally. Our recent international results prove that conclusively. And the fault lies with the basic mistake made by the SRU in the general policy they adopt with the clubs. Their view – put simply – is that if they could broaden the base of Scottish rugby, they could build the pyramid higher. My own argument is that if you get things right at the top, the rest of the game looks after itself.

The trouble is that there are far too many mediocre teams in the Leagues – even in the First Division where Gala and Hawick have dominated apart from the year in which Heriots snatched the title. Those – and a couple of others – can realistically expect never to be relegated but there are at least four who start every season knowing that it's going to be a struggle to survive. They need better players and we should take a leaf out of the Welsh book in order to make sure they get them.

There they have a well-established feeder system. It works like this. If, for example, Cardiff suddenly find that Terry Holmes is injured and they need another scrum-half, they send their representatives out into the valleys to find a scrum-half from a smaller club to cover for him. They make no bones about it and the scheme works well for everyone. The small club knows that one of its players is gaining extra experience which he will bring back to it. Cardiff are able consistently to put out good sides at the highest level and Welsh rugby generally benefits.

But that doesn't happen in Scotland at all. If Jordanhill went to Glasgow High – in the Third Division – and asked for someone 'on loan' the answer would come back 'Why?' But to leave a good player going nowhere is a loss to him and to Scottish Rugby. John Beattie, who managed to force his way into the 1980 British Lions squad for South Africa while playing in the Third Division for Glasgow Accies, is the exception which proves the rule. The better example is Ian Paxton of Glenrothes in the Sixth Division. For his club, he is running in try after try – but when he steps up, he wonders why, in a 'B' international, he is getting tired in the second half and being knocked about. The answer is that he is playing in a standard which is too low for him and he is picking up all kinds of bad habits.

Now if the system were right, Paxton, a number eight, should be stepping up the ladder a rung or two at a time and going to the club where his talents – and he has lots of them – will be tested in the real heat of battle. The way forward for the Leagues is to concentrate the best players at the top. Gala, as I've said before, aren't afraid to call in players from all over the place to give themselves a consistently strong side. They're known as the Scottish Co-optimists and the joke was that when the Boat People arrived at Leith Docks from Vietnam, their committee was there to meet them.

They brought in all kinds – Nairn, Jim Aitken, Tom Smith, Eddie Henderson – the list is almost endless. And the proof of the pudding was when they won the Championship. Bringing

31

on good players by getting them to top teams is an urgent priority if we are to make proper use of our talents. Put it this way, if the Second Division isn't five yards faster than the third and the First Division five yards faster than the second, then there's something radically wrong. I would like to see Scottish Selectors forget about anyone who isn't playing in the two top Leagues. Indeed maybe they should concentrate solely on Division One. That would give the good guys an incentive to go and establish themselves.

The other problem with the Leagues is that the fixtures sometimes work out unfairly. Take Langholm when they were relegated in 1979. It turned out that four of their first five games were away from home to Melrose, Watsonians, Hawick and Haddington. They were down before they had a chance to even things up by using their own ground advantage.

So what would my perfect season be? I think it should start with a couple of warm-up matches – and then there should be ten straight League games (I'd have eleven clubs in each Division). After that there would be district matches in a new format leading onto the international period of the season where clubs would play friendly matches between the games in the Five Nations Tournament. This would allow the traditional non-league fixtures to be played while the Scottish players could take something of a breather. The end of the season should be put aside for Jubilee Games, Sevens and the general run of fun rugby. And every summer, a full Scotland side or a 'B' team should be sent on tour to keep the team spirit, the camaraderie and consistency in selection going.

I knew I was going places in rugby when I was called into the Glasgow side in 1962. District rugby in Scotland is the equivalent of England's County Championship. To the player it's a sign that he is moving towards the greatest honour of all, a dark blue jersey. It's a shame that some of the people who have run Glasgow over the years haven't taken it as seriously as they should.

They've never gone out and arranged a proper fixture list. They've never taken us on a short tour at the start of a season to get the boys together. Some of their selections have bordered upon the ludicrous. Certain clubs always seemed to have had players in the side regardless of how good or bad they were. The training and preparation for games was, to say the least, haphazard. Sometimes we didn't even know when or where to turn up. What could be a great force for improvement in the Scottish game has been impeded through sheer amateurism.

Scotland is divided up into four rugby districts. The South, traditionally the strongest who pick their players from the Border clubs; Edinburgh, who fluctuate; Glasgow, which does the same, and the North and Midlands, the Cinderellas, who don't have many top clubs and who find it difficult to train because of the distances involved.

They play each other in the Championship and also arrange games against the English Counties and occasional forays abroad. And that's where I make my first criticism of the way Glasgow rugby has been run. If district rugby is to be taken seriously we need more quality fixtures. At the moment our only regular fixture outside the Championship is against Lancashire – and even that's played in midweek, an arrangement I am totally against. Any Wednesday match at this level is an imposition on players who have to get up and earn their living the next morning. The last time we came back from playing the English County Champions at Orrel it was five o'clock in the morning before I was in bed. And I'm expected to be up bright-eyed and bushy-tailed facing a class of youngsters first thing in the morning.

I don't see why the Glasgow committee doesn't try and get games – Saturday games – against top quality club sides all over Great Britain. Imagine how our standards would have to improve if we knew we were facing Swansea or Llanelli, Moseley or Leicester. Instead we are content with the way we are.

Why doesn't anyone consider the possibility of the Scottish Districts taking part in the English County Championship itself? Under my plans there would be time enough during the season to fit in such matches, right in that period between the end of the League season and the start of the Internationals.

On top of all the other good points, such games would do away with the need for a final trial – firstly because Scottish selectors would have had plenty of opportunity to see prospective internationals performing near the top of the tree; secondly because, at that level, rugby is a pressure game. It's about learning all there is to know about your job and then finding out how well you can do it by testing yourself against the best players in your own country, in the rest of the British Isles and eventually – if you're good enough – in the rest of the world. And it's about doing that every time you go on to the pitch. Individual consistency and team consistency are the most valuable commodities of all in winning rugby.

As far as selections are concerned, I've been Glasgow captain for more years than I'd like to remember and I still don't understand the way the committee thinks. Sometimes I don't think they know themselves. In 1976 we were due to play the South and the previous weekend Jim Carswell and Wes Wyroslawski were injured in Jordanhill's game against Hawick. At the training session on the Sunday, I went out of my way as captain to inform the secretary that there was no way they could play forty-eight hours later on the Tuesday. But for reasons best known to himself he decided not to act on that piece of information and so, on the morning of the game, there was a mad scramble around to find some replacements.

The trouble was that the guy who should have stood in for Wes worked on a building site and there was no way that he could be contacted at short notice. So they pulled in a player who, with the best will in the world, just wasn't up to this standard of rugby. I think he knew it himself and he certainly did his best.

However, the upshot was that we went down 42–0 and it wasn't entirely the fault of either stand-in; no side loses by that many simply because a couple of players are missing. But the fact that the whole team was muttering about the selectors' incompetence didn't exactly improve morale.

I could take up the rest of the book naming other instances of this kind of careless work by the Glasgow committee. I often felt I wasn't getting much back for all the effort I was putting in for the District. Once, my Jordanhill teammate Richie

Dixon and I travelled up from our homes in Edinburgh to St Andrews for a game against the North and Midlands and were due to meet up with the side for tea. I rang up the Glasgow secretary to find out which hotel we were all gathering at but he was on holiday and no one seemed to know. Eventually – and a bit late – we did bump into the rest of the squad. It's a small point but small points can make all the difference between winning and losing at any sport.

In my last season, Glasgow were due to play the South at Hughenden, one of the top Glasgow grounds. Because of the frosty weather the game was transferred to Murrayfield, protected by its famous electric blanket, and the decision was taken at ten o'clock in the morning. But the players were still not expected to turn up until 12.30 for a two o'clock kick-off in Edinburgh. And they were only there *that* early because I had asked them to be, in the hope that we could have a chat and a proper time to change. Instead there was a mad dash across country to Edinburgh, we changed in the coach as it went past Turnhouse Airport and we arrived at Murrayfield two minutes before the kick-off.

Needless to say, Glasgow lost. And not too many players enhanced their reputations in what was an unofficial Scottish trial. Another man wasn't too happy either. Referee Brian Anderson, who lives in Edinburgh, hadn't been informed of the switch and had travelled through to Glasgow to find the ground deserted. That day was a wasted journey for a lot of people.

Nothing sums up the small-mindedness of the committee more than their attitude to money – or rather, expenses. Take one of the times we went down to play Lancashire. It was a very important game for us because there was the old England v. Scotland needle involved quite apart from anything else. We were going down the M6 in the coach when the official in charge stood up at the front and said, 'OK lads, we are stopping at the next motorway café. Have anything you like to eat – up to 30p.' A cup of coffee was 20p. We just sat there and didn't know whether to laugh or cry.

Then there was the general question of my travel expenses. Living in Edinburgh, it's quite expensive playing for Glasgow, the team I must represent because of my club qualification. The trip from my house to the usual training ground and back is over a hundred miles. According to Glasgow, they pay mileage expenses on the basis of thirty miles to the gallon. As it happens I drive an old estate car because it's good for piling in my three sons – Andrew, Ross and Scott – and all their gear on holiday. So I claimed £4 for petrol at the current prices. They replied that under their formula I was only due £2.70 – and that's what I got. They didn't take into consideration that I was bringing other members of the side through with me. And one last point on Glasgow expenses. They don't pay them out until the end of the season, but you still have to submit them on a match-to-match basis otherwise you are not eligible for a penny. So outgoings which you could have incurred in November aren't paid out until the following May.

I'd add that the SRU attitude is quite different. They always pay out on the spot. But then, there's all the difference between night and day between the two bodies.

'I belong to Glasgow,' says the song. But sometimes Glasgow was off-key.

# 5

# The Auld Enemy

I had – by 1969 – given up all hope of ever playing for Scotland. I'd had my first trial way back in 1962 and after it one of the selectors had come up and said to me: 'If only you were a couple of inches taller, you would walk into the side. As it is . . .' What difference does a couple of inches make either way? I thought to myself, and became resigned to the fact that my rugby career would be played out for Jordanhill and Glasgow.

Size doesn't matter. The most important qualifications for propping are strength and technique. By regular weight training I had built myself up to over 14 stone and eight years in club rugby had taught me most of the tricks of the trade. I don't think any of the guys I had propped against would have dismissed me on the grounds that I was only five foot nine. They knew better.

But my lack of inches surprised many people. At that first trial our captain was Mike Campbell Lammerton of London Scottish. On the morning of the game he gathered the side around him and asked those of us who did not know him to make our introductions, from fullback to forward. He kept looking at me rather nervously when he found out I wasn't a threequarter. He already knew the half-back pair of Brian Simmers and Tremayne Rodd, so realized I must be a forward. Lammerton, that giant six foot six lock, finally asked, 'What position do you play in?'

'Prop.'

'Which side?'

'Loose head.'

'Thank God I don't have to get underneath you. I'm playing on the other side,' he said.

So short of buying myself a medieval rack and stretching myself three inches I couldn't see much hope of ever playing for Scotland. And, aged twenty-six, married to Eileen and father of a five-month-old son Andrew, my mind was turning in different directions – away from rugby and on to a new love: skiing.

I was earning a few bob at weekends taking kids up to Glenshee and was missing the occasional game for Jordanhill. As a newly married man with a mortgage I rather needed the dough. It never dawned on me that my rugby career was about to take off.

I was up in Glenshee, at Glenkilrie Lodge with a group of boys from Barmulloch College in Glasgow when the telephone went. We had been out on the mountains. The call came from my boss at school, John Blain. 'Stop skiing immediately,' he said. At first I thought he was referring to some problems with the insurance for the boys; because the sport was still considered hazardous at that time and we had taken out policies to cover them against any accident. I asked what the problem was.

'Nothing to do with that,' he said. 'The boys can carry on skiing. It's just you who've got to stop. You're playing against England on Saturday week.'

All I remember about the next few days – and the match itself – was the complete excitement of it all. Here was I, a hick from the sticks, about to play for Scotland at Twickenham. The biggest crowd I had played in front of before was about 5000 for a match between the Combined Cities and Australia at Hughenden. Here there would be 65,000 and the noise would be deafening.

I was due to meet up with Sandy Carmichael – to start what was to become one of the most famous International partnerships in Scottish rugby – and a selector, the inimitable Hamish Kemp. It was the first time I had flown and the day was wet and windy. I couldn't have picked a worse couple to fly with because they were both as nervous as kittens. By the time we arrived at Heathrow, I felt I'd undertaken just about the most difficult journey since Columbus discovered America.

On the Thursday Jim Telfer, the captain, led us through a training session only hours after I had arrived. There wasn't much time for congratulations before we were hard at work at Richmond preparing for the game against the Auld Enemy.

I'd heard a lot about the Englishman I was to face: Keith Fairbrother of Coventry. By all accounts he was supposed to be a mixture of Superman and the Incredible Hulk. However, at that time I felt I could have walked on water so it didn't matter too much. I couldn't wait for Saturday and that journey to Twickenham, a place I had never seen in my life before.

I suppose I must have been nervous. Five times I checked my bag to see if I had forgotten anything. But the boots, the shorts and socks, towel, the jock strap, the mouthguard were all there.

We arrived at Twickenham an hour before kick-off, walked down the tunnel and up the four steps on to the pitch. I've seen people freeze up, I've seen others who couldn't stop talking as they tried to overcome their nerves. But for me the feeling was one of complete exhilaration. I couldn't wait to get back up the tunnel, into the dressing room and look at the row of blue jerseys hanging on pegs. In case the selectors changed their minds, I grabbed it, and pulled it down over my shoulders. From that moment on, I never thought of myself as anything but a Scottish player.

I was in and out of the toilet a few times, but that was nothing unusual. Meanwhile the noise was building up outside and heightening the tension I was feeling going into the game. Jim Telfer gave the pep-talk, with special words of encouragement to myself and Billy Steele, the other new cap. 'Open the doors,' I thought; 'Let me on to that pitch.' I wanted to see this man mountain called Fairbrother.

At last, we were there. Up the tunnel and onto the grass. Fairbrother didn't seem too awesome a character at all. I knew I wouldn't let Scotland down. I kept remembering Dickie's words of advice. 'Just knock them down. And I mean down – *dead*.'

There wasn't a fairytale ending. We lost 8–3 but I had been initiated into the Big League. Perhaps I wouldn't have won any Man of the Match award but I felt I had done my bit, the only sour point being that we hadn't won. I went on to the banquet at the Hilton Hotel that night thinking: 'If this is International Rugby, it's where I want to be.'

To be honest I'd rather beat Wales than England. I mean the Welsh are so bloody cocky about their rugby and it's good to take them down a peg or two. Wales happen to be the best as well. Throughout the Seventies we managed to beat England quite regularly. So it wasn't quite such a big thing to win the Calcutta Cup match either at Twickenham or Murrayfield.

The trouble with English rugby is that there's too much of it. It's like three different countries rolled into one. In the West, at places like Bristol and Gloucester, they play a type of game which is very similar to that in Wales. That's not surprising because the clubs have a lot of fixtures in the valleys.

As Dave Rollitt says, 'Show me a man who gets into his car in Bristol and drives to Pontypool on a wet Wednesday night just to have his balls kicked in, and I will show you a man who is a devotee of rugby.'

Then there are the North and the Midlands clubs, who play a hard brand of the game as well. And then there's London, the soft South. And it always seemed to me that an England side in the past had players in it just because they belonged to this club or that club. There always seemed to be a Harlequin, for example.

At last they seem to have got it right. Their Grand Slam this year was achieved in fine style. They based their team on the best county, Lancashire, and I take my hat off to Billy Beaumont, Fran Cotton, Tony Neary and Co.

I was brought up like any good Scottish child to believe that the English, as a people, were quiet, gentle and inoffensive, the sort of race which wouldn't say boo to a goose. Once every two years Tarbolton emptied while the men went off to watch Scotland smash the English out of sight at Wembley and came back with incredible stories of how small the whisky measures were, and how the English seemed happy to hold on to half a pint all night.

If they'd ever met that man Rollitt or Nigel Horton or Fran or Billy, they would have thought again. The English can dish it out with the best of them.

Big Alistair McHarg tells the story of playing for London Scottish against Moseley in 1969 just before Nigel won his first cap. He thought he would give him a dress rehearsal of what to expect against the Scots. But before Al could get off the mark, he was lying flat on his back having been on the end of a warning shot from this skinny Englishman called 'Orton. After about five minutes of to-ing and fro-ing the referee decided enough was enough and both men were happy to call it a draw.

I've come to have a great respect for the English, as tourists and rugby players in their own right. Mind you, I would remind them of my record against England. Played ten, won five, lost four, drawn one.

Two years after my first visit to Twickenham I was back again in the first Scottish side to win there since the War. Our 16–15 victory saw us back in the dressing rooms in a state of complete euphoria . . . but we were soon brought down to earth when we got back to the hotel and one of the committee came up and said, 'I'd rather have lost than used the tactics that were going on out there today.'

I admit it was one of the hardest matches between the two countries and the rucking got a wee bit strong at times. It led to tempers getting frayed and a few punches being thrown. That didn't make it a dirty game: it was just that the score see-sawed back and forward throughout the match and the commitment was 150 per cent about getting the ball. With a guy like Horton about, a man who doesn't know what a backward step is, the battle was bound to get a bit towsy. That wasn't the first time and it won't be the last in which that's happened. It was a question of getting stuck in and what that committee man didn't know was that there were no hard feelings among the players afterwards. One Fleet Street rugby writer blamed me for starting the whole business and called me a 'Poison Dwarf'. I took it as a great compliment.

The English players, coming off the field, said, 'Well done, you wee bastard.' And together we all enjoyed a night which wore on till the early hours.

The match itself all depended upon the last kick. I had a hand in the try which brought us to within one point of England deep in injury time. We got a short penalty and I took the ball on the run, heading straight for the English forwards. Fran Cotton stuck out his arm and I ran straight into it. But I managed to lay the ball back; the Scottish pack went straight over me and fed the ball for Chris Rea to shoot over the line. So it all·rested on P.C. – captain Peter Brown – with the conversion.

If ever there was a man who wasn't going to miss a conversion at a moment like this it was the good P.C. They could have put the entire 70,000 crowd right round the ball and he would just have clocked out and got on with it. P.C. put the ball down, blew his nose, turned his back, then ran up and hit it straight between the posts.

We had rattled the English – and at the right time. A week later we were due to play England at Murrayfield in a centenary game to celebrate the 100th year of matches between the two countries. After the match, David Powell, the Northampton man I had been propping against, came up and said: 'We don't play like that.' 'Well,' I replied, 'you've seven days to learn.'

We hadn't just rattled them, we had put them in a state of total panic. In the next game, it was a complete shambles for them as we coasted home in front of our own crowd 26–6. Hamish Kemp said afterwards – and he wasn't joking: 'We let them off the hook.' England's troubles started even before the match began because when they turned up at Murrayfield they had forgotten their strip. There were alarm stations and someone had to go back to the North British hotel so that they didn't take the field starkers.

P.C.'s team talk was magnificent: 'We beat these so-and-so's on their own pitch last week. This time it's our own people out there, thousands of them. Go down the tunnel and look at the flags. They all belong to us. Let's go and trample them again.' After that call to arms it had to be a Scottish win.

We scored five tries: Bill Dickinson was, of course, the, coach and that further put down the myth that we played ten-man rugby. I was directly involved in one of the scores, setting up a ruck which allowed Billy Steele to run in on the blind side. What I remember is the vast amount of possession we won and the amount of running the backs did with the ball.

Those two games – and those two great wins in eight days – were the start of the great renaissance in Scottish Rugby during that period and mostly it was based on what came to be known as the Mean Machine, a front five who hefted about two tons across the pitch and which could outscrummage anything in the world. There was Sandy and myself, Gordon Brown and Al McHarg, the four corner posts of that structure. And as hooker either Quinton Dunlop, who played in those two matches, Bobby Clark, Duncan Madsen or Colin Fisher all had spells in the middle.

No wonder Edward Heath, addressing the banquet after the centenary international, said, 'I am lucky that I can address you not as an Englishman but as Prime Minister of Great Britain.' The double-header was the turning point for the side that Dickie was pulling together and for the men in it. Scotland was, quite rightly, beginning to stir.

In 1972, we were going for a third consecutive Calcutta Cup win and a fourth victory over England on the trot. Sandy Carmichael, Gordon Brown, Roger Arneill and myself had all toured New Zealand with the British Lions in the meantime and with the pack also containing P.C., Alistair McHarg and Nairn McEwan we were extremely confident. As it turned out P.C. just about beat them on his own. He scored 13 points including a try at just the right time. It meant that in the successful spell against the English he had scored 34 points including three tries.

I was captain in 1973 when Scotland headed for Twickenham again and this time the game was trebly important. We were seeking the Triple Crown for the first time since 1938. Much happened before that game and for a solid week McLauchlan wiped Rangers and Celtic off the top of the sports pages. The whole country was worried about my broken leg.

Three weeks before, against Ireland, I had been injured. It was a very simple thing. Barry McGann, the Irish fly-half, came round the blindside and I closed him down. Barry put a little grub kick forward and I had a chance to fall on the ball and kill it. Instead I tried to nudge it into touch and as Barry followed up, we went down together and he ended up sitting on my leg. All a complete accident.

At first I didn't think too much about it. It seemed like a bruise. I went into the next few scrummages without any problems but running was difficult. Eventually our trainer Jock Brown came on and squirted some of that freezing painkiller over the lower leg and ankle. It was quite useless. The doctor, Donald McLeod, took a look but I told him not to touch it and carried on playing. Ten minutes later I knew that I would have to go off. When I got to the touchline, it was clear that Donald knew fine well that the leg was broken – and was furious that I had risked further injury by staying on the field. There was no chance that the break would become worse but I had damaged the muscular tissue surrounding it.

In the stands my wife didn't know a thing. Eileen had gone out of the stand at half-time and when she came back someone sitting in the next seat told her that I had broken my leg. She wasn't upset. That was the way I would have wanted it.

They took me from Murrayfield to the Royal Infirmary in a police car and whipped me straight into the X-ray theatre. A young house doctor looked at the plates and said, 'You've no chance of playing this year.' 'Well,' I said, 'that's not too bad; there's only a month left of the season.' 'I don't mean that. I mean you won't play for the rest of 1973.'

They brought a top specialist along and he asked when my next big match was: 'England in three weeks' time.' 'No problem,' he said, 'just as long as you put yourself in my hands and do everything I say. And I mean everything.' I nearly jumped out of bed with delight. They put some splints on the leg, handed me a pair of crutches and off I set to make the speech at the banquet. I must say I rather enjoyed that

Ayr Academy First XV, 1958-59. Standing (*left to right*): A. J. Smith, A. Ewen, R. A. A. Johnson, R. Colquhoun, C. G. B. Melrose, J. B. Houston (vice-captain), A. McGiven, S. Kerr. Seated (*left to right*): N. Provan, A. S. McHarg (treasurer), J. D. Cairns Esq (rector), M. H. Denness (captain), T. B. Watson Esq (games master), I. McLauchlan, I. Hay (secretary). Front row: A. Caldwell (*left*) and J. A. Wilson

My first cap against England in 1969 – preparing to tackle Dave Rollitt

On the way to that try in the first Test, New Zealand, 1971

Above left: Putting the shoulder to the Lions wheel . . . against Northern Transvaal in 1974

Above right: Homecoming. Back from South Africa and Andrew, Scott, Ross and Eileen are waiting

Below: Offering succour to Gareth. Against Eastern Province, 1974

One way to gain a few extra inches. P. C. and Nairn McEwan hold me aloft

The best British Lions team ever. Preparing for the first Test against South Africa, 1974

Almost a scrum half

Scottish XV, Murrayfield, 3 February 1973. Standing (*left to right*): M. F. Palmade (referee), C. M. Telfer, G. M. Strachan, A. F. McHarg, I. W. Forsyth, J. G Millican, A. R. Irvine, J. Young (touch judge). Seated (*left to right*): I. R. McGeechan, D. Shedden, P. C. Brown, I. McLauchlan (captain), A. B. Carmichael, R. L. Clark, N. A. MacEwan. Front row: W. C. C. Steele (*left*) and D. W. Morgan

Alan Lawson passes. Two England men, discarded far too soon, go for the ball – Tony Neary and Alan Old

Skippering the British Lions on a muddy day in South Africa against the Combined Universities. Broonie looks on as Sandy is grounded

You can't keep two good Scots down. Broonie and myself

The Mafia in South Africa, 1974. Standing: Fergus Slattery (*left*) and Syd Millar
Seated (*left to right*): self, Coet Wisser and Willie John McBride

Roger Uttley and Andy Ripley set the pace

banquet because I had the best possible excuse to sit there and get jugged up without Eileen gently nagging me for the next dance.

I had to give it ten days for the break to calcify and the specialist had told me to rest, relax and do nothing. I went into school and taught with my foot propped up on the desk. Then I was given permission to start running about again and I trained very hard to get ready for Twickenham.

I felt fit, I really did. The only problem was that I was still limping. When the Scottish team arrived in London on the Thursday I trained with the others but this infuriating limp was still there. I knew it wouldn't affect my performance but the chairman of the selectors, Lex Govan, said, understandably, that the committee were worried. I pleaded with him to let me have a painkilling injection the next day and train again. He agreed.

On the Friday, Lex spoke to me again. He asked if I felt fit. I told him I was – and that was that. I would captain Scotland three weeks after breaking my leg. We were all very happy.

We lost 20–13. Afterwards, with the Triple Crown chance now gone, the inquest opened on whether or not I should have played. Let me make two points. Firstly I wasn't the only one carrying an injury at Twickenham that day. Alistair McHarg, for example, wasn't completely fit. And my injury had nothing to do with the defeat. We made mistakes, England punished them and in that class of rugby such errors are usually fatal.

I took the precaution of wearing *two* polystyrene shin-pads because I sensed there would be quite of lot of Englishmen queuing up to take a kick at me and I didn't want them to know which leg was giving the trouble. Propping against Fran Cotton, such a precaution seemed eminently worthwhile.

In the match England were eight points up in jig time with David Duckham running through our side almost straight from the kick-off. We were always behind, despite a Billy Steele try out of nothing and the truth is that we beat ourselves because of the mistakes. The famous McLauchlan leg had nothing to do with it.

I thought the English captain John Pullin was a trifle out of order at the dinner when he said 'I thought that Scotland would have done us the honour of fielding a fit side.' That wasn't the case at all. The remark disappointed me.

On the overall question of whether I should have played or not, I give the same answer now as then. Of course I should. I thought the selectors showed tremendous courage in picking me. It would have been much easier for them to have left me out. Generally, though, the player shouldn't be left to decide on whether he can compete or not.

Any international cap worth his salt thinks that even if he's only half fit he'll do a better job than the guy sitting on the bench. I know that I was injured in the fourth Test against South Africa the next year but it never dawned on me to leave the field. You have to possess a conceit about yourself to succeed. I remember Sandy Carmichael getting hurt against France in Paris when I was sitting on the bench and was absolutely furious that he wouldn't quit and let me into the side when he was a passenger. But although I was furious I understood exactly why he wanted to stay on. I would have done precisely the same if the roles had been reversed.

On fitness generally I would operate this rule as a coach. If a man isn't fit enough to take part in the Sunday squad session on the week of the match, he shouldn't play on the Saturday either. But that Triple Crown, I repeat, wasn't lost because I played with a broken leg. I would do the same thing all over again and know that I wasn't letting myself or the side down. Quite the reverse.

If that disappointment was acute, we evened it up in 1974 when another win over the English was one of the high water marks of Dickie's years as coach. The Mean Machine was going well and we were always confident of winning at Murrayfield. Away our record wasn't so good, but with the Saltires waving and the huge crowds, we didn't reckon anyone could beat us there.

This time we lived dangerously. England made one incredible mistake. They gave Alan Old just one kick at goal and he kicked it. Fullback Peter Rossborough had about ten attempts and missed the lot. Why that was allowed to happen remains a complete mystery. We should have won rather more easily despite a refereeing break that went against us. Colin Telfer took a tapped penalty just outside our 25 and ran at the English forwards, who hadn't retreated ten yards. Tony Neary didn't wait for the whistle – rightly so. He tackled Colin, drove forward and England scored.

In the end it all rested on an Andy Irvine penalty in the last minute, struck right through the middle of the posts from forty-five yards. That gave us the 16–14 win, and people ask, 'Was that a better pressure kick than P.C.'s at Twickenham in 1971?' I think not. P.C. knew that his was absolutely the last chance and it may have looked deceptively simple on TV but it was anything but that. Andy, simply, is a tremendous kicker and his kick at Murrayfield was just a tremendous kick.

A year later in 1975, we were chasing the Triple Crown yet again after wins against Wales and Ireland. This was to be the zenith of the Mean Machine – and the defeat, 7–6, was the hardest to take. It was never quite the same after that. I still get depressed when I think how near we came to winning and what that would have done for Scottish Rugby. It could have set us up for years. But it didn't work out that way.

It was a hard game by anyone's standards. Our pack was at its best and there was a lot of sorting out to do. We were upset when Nairn had his jaw broken in a collision with Tony Neary. Ian Barnes came into the second row, Al McHarg moved back to number eight and that upset us a bit.

David Rollitt had a great game for England. What a man he was, just about the most difficult competitor to play against. He was into everything. I'll never understand why England gave him the bullet years before his time. They did the same thing with Neary and Peter Dixon. Anyway the sorting out was considerable and Billy Steele got his ear cut in one bout of it.

We were leading 6–3. We were getting masses of good ball but doing nothing with it. It was all so frustrating. Then came the English try. Alan Morley chased an aimless ball through, Andy Irvine let it bounce and it went behind him over the line. It became a chase between the two of them and to this day Andy claims he touched the ball down first. I've seen the replays a hundred times and come to the conclusion that neither man actually got to it. The ball bounced away from the pair of them and there was no touch down at all.

That put England into the lead and I think the referee gave us a couple of penalties to make amends. I asked Dougie Morgan to take them both and he missed. That was extraordinary because there isn't a more reliable place-kicker than Dougie. He couldn't believe it when the second went wide. It was a bitter, bitter defeat because that was *the* Scottish team. We had been playing as a side for the last four or five years and were more or less all automatic choices. That meant that players could express themselves and the spirit was high. There were no cliques, no jealousies and we felt we deserved that Triple Crown. I remember that night we went to the dance and hung about saying nothing and feeling hellish. But there were no recriminations, no pointing of fingers at guys, no blaming of anyone because we had lost. It was that sort of side. Afterwards it was never quite the same. New players arrived, the team started to break up and the results were never as good. It was the bitterest pill of them all.

We won at Murrayfield the next year, 1976, as England went through one of their periodic selection upheavals, discarding experienced players and bringing in newcomers. The match is clouded in my memory; maybe I was still thinking of what might have been – what could have been – the year before.

# 6

# The First Tours

I sometimes wake up in the middle of the night in a cold sweat, thinking how close I came to ending my international career almost before it started. Instead of touring New Zealand and South Africa with the British Lions, I could easily have been found back home in Scotland, on the ski-slopes of Glenshee and Aviemore. As I've said, there was a moment when I was ready to give up rugby altogether and change to a new sport.

Touring has now become part of my life. It's brought me the best friends I have in the world and rugby has given me all the experiences which I can fondly look back on in my old age. The laughs, the fun, the parties and playing the game at the highest levels are all privileges I won't forget in a hurry. But they very nearly never happened.

In 1969, after gaining my first cap – against England at Twickenham – I went off to South America as part of Scotland's squad against the Pumas of Argentina. A year later we went the other way round the world to Australia. And after those two experiences I was ready to pack it in altogether. In a word, they were both disasters. And after them I needed a fair bit of persuasion to carry on.

Argentina, at least, was an experience. Scotland undertook a six-match tour with only twenty-one players. That soon became twenty players as the Gala forward Ken Oliver couldn't shake off a calf muscle injury he got before we even set foot on the aeroplane.

Four days after arriving in Buenos Aires, Ken was on his way back home again – and we had to do the best we could.

And we ran right into the rough stuff. Every game on the

49

tour was physical. But why beat about the bush? Every game was dirty. The Argentinians are big strong lads and didn't need to play it that way. In fairness they've changed since, but at that time they were into just about everything, and the refereeing, to put it politely, was indifferent. They had their own version of the straight-arm tackle, or clothesline as it's called. They didn't just stick out their arm for you to run into, they swung it at you.

There's not a lot you can do to protect yourself against that sort of foul. You don't get enough time to see it coming. But that's not all. They had never heard of the offside law and if the offside law isn't observed, you just don't have proper rugby. Add to that early tackles and late tackles and you have a Black Museum of all that's wrong in the game.

Anyway, it was my first tour and I was determined to prove myself as an internationalist. And I'm not exactly one to run away when the going gets a wee bit rough. It wasn't so much the rugby which turned me off; it was the constant socializing, a lot of the time with people who had little or no interest in what you had to say to them.

On later tours, managements realized that players don't want to be standing around nibbling at little things on sticks and sipping the occasional orange juice. Your hosts are quite happy if a couple of the players turn up at the reception so that the duties can be shared round. But in Argentina it was a case of 'One in, the lot in.' At times it was farcical.

For example, we arrived in Rosario for a match, only to find that there was a fullscale civil war going on, and a twenty-four hour strike that had led to rioting all over the city. Our bus driver wouldn't go near the place. He dumped us at a country club about twenty miles out and we rang for taxis to take us into the hotel. Eventually, the local Rugby Union supplied them and they set off at about eighty miles-an-hour, knocking down everything that stood in the way as we raced in past factories that were burning to the ground. The hotel was surrounded by troops and there were palls of smoke all over the town.

A few of us – game for anything – walked up to the roof of the hotel to get a grandstand view of the rioting. A couple of minutes later, the hotel manager came storming up, pointed to the helicopters whirring above us and shouted: 'For Christ sake get down, they'll think you're snipers.' At least I think that's what he said; we didn't understand a word of Spanish. We just got the message.

The rioting had put a stop to the workers erecting temporary grandstands for the match and the locals asked us if we would agree to a twenty-four hour postponement. Lex Govan, the manager, agreed. Good for Lex. Then he announced that we all had to go to a reception about two blocks away despite the fact that you could hear gunfire all over the place.

'Look,' he said: 'We'd better not all go at once. The safest way is to go in twos and look bloody sharp about it.' Imagine, scurrying through a war zone for a few gin-and-tonics. At least, gin-and-tonics for the management. We weren't allowed to drink.

We mopped up all the provincial opposition along the way and *en route* to the second Test against the Pumas – in front of a 20,000 crowd in B.A. – we didn't expect too much trouble. What we didn't realize was that the entire Argentinian squad had been down in Mar del Plata for three weeks training just for this match. They were idolized and they gave us a lot of trouble.

It was really nasty. If they weren't straight-arming us, the crowd were throwing pennies at us. We managed to win 6–3 but it was a score that never was which sticks in my mind. We were under pressure, kicked upfield with ten minutes left and their wing forward caught the ball, shouted 'Mark' and in the same breath kicked just about the best drop goal I've ever seen, from about fifty yards. The ball whistled between the posts and we thought 'That's that.' But the referee had already given the mark – much to his own annoyance, I think – and when the lad took it again, he could only trundle the next drop thirty yards along the floor. Someone picked it up – gratefully – and booted it upfield. The only real question left to be answered was whether we could make it into the dressing rooms at the final whistle before the crowd got to us. We did.

There was a strange sequel to all the nastiness. At the

banquet that night, Jim Telfer, our skipper, gave the traditional speech. You wouldn't expect a Borderer to mince his
words and Jim tore straight in: 'I've never seen such dirty
rugby in all my life,' he said: 'Unless you cut out the filth,
you'll never get anyone to come here and play you; you'll
never be a real rugby country.' And so on for about ten
minutes.

Jim sat down, the interpreter stood up and translated it into
Spanish, taking only ten seconds. The doctor sitting next to
me explained that all he had used out of the captain's speech
was a brief reference to how wonderful the country was. He
hadn't bothered to mention the serious points.

The whole experience wasn't for me. Jim had done a
tremendous job on the field, never shirking a tackle. And off
the field he had stopped the mumping among players. But the
best joke of the trip summed up what kind of a tour it had
been. 'When we started the bus went to the daily training
session and the taxi took the injured players to the doctors. At
the end it was the other way round.' I didn't cry when I left
Argentina.

The next year, 1970, it was Australia. The tour started on a
very sad personal note because two weeks before the start my
father died. I debated whether to call if off but Eileen helped
to persuade me that there wasn't much point in staying at
home. Earlier that year Scotland had dropped me after the
18–9 defeat by Wales in Cardiff. I didn't like being singled out
as a scapegoat but that's part of the game and you've got to
accept it. I went to Australia determined to win my place
back.

The tour was fated from the start. We flew from London
and on take-off from Amsterdam, the plane hit some birds and
we went straight back to Heathrow, losing a whole day. Our
manager Hector Munro, later to be President of the SRU and
Minister of Sport in Margaret Thatcher's Government, had to
fly back again early in the tour to fight an election and that left
George Burrell, his assistant, in charge.

Managing any tour side isn't easy. Apart from the general
administration and the problems of moving a large group of
players about, there is the constant round of socializing and

speechmaking. A manager's work is never done. He's constantly sifting through dozens of invitations, and dealing with a hundred and one unseen tasks. He has to arrange medical treatment if required, meals, visits.

Of all the managers on tours, Doug Smith in New Zealand in 1971 was the man most on top of the job and he had Carwyn James to look after the playing side. When Hector Munro went, George Burrell had to do the lot, which is asking too much of anyone. And he didn't have a group of senior players who could have helped him out.

Frank Laidlaw of Melrose was captain and was too nice a guy for the job. He had missed only one Scottish game since first being capped in 1965 and he was a great hooker. But he wasn't the sort of man to crack the whip as Jim Telfer had done in the Argentine. To make matters worse, Tom Elliot and Sid Smith were injured in the first match and with the queue for the taxi to the doctor's lengthening all the time, we were permanently under strength. So much so that I had to play hooker as a replacement for Derek Deans in the Sydney match.

Those injuries meant that we couldn't come up with any overall team plan and we got increasingly unhappy about the refereeing standards. When we were beaten in Queensland the penalty count was nineteen against us, four against the Aussies. Every time we managed to get near their line, the ref would award a penalty and they would clear. We would spend the next few minutes getting back to the same position and it would start all over again. Either we were being very stupid giving away all these penalties or the referee was keeping more of an eye on us than the opposition. When I went back the next year, the same thing happened with the same referee.

We got to Sydney for the Test completely demoralized after a beating along the way by New South Wales and with a crushing injury burden. Frankie limped on to the pitch; he could hardly walk. Sandy Carmichael wasn't much better and Peter Stagg was hurt as well. But the nearest I got was a place in the stands as a possible replacement for all eight forward positions. We got a drubbing 23–3.

So, on the way home I began thinking. I had still retained

that interest in skiing. I was enjoying taking the kids up to the hills on Duke of Edinburgh Award schemes and the money would still have been useful. I was really ready to quit.

To rub salt into the wound, on the way home the plane broke down in Bahrain. I was in a pretty morose mood and poured my heart out to one of my friends on the trip, the fly-half Ian Robertson. He said this had been the worst possible tour. Nothing could be as bad again. He advised me to stick with it and twelve months later I was heading round the world again as a British Lion on my way to conquer the All Blacks. Thanks for the advice, pal.

# 7

# New Zealand 1971

'Welcome to the Slaughterhouse.' Those were the first words anyone spoke to me on New Zealand soil. To be strictly accurate they weren't spoken on New Zealand soil, rather on New Zealand tarmac, just a few yards from the plane which had brought the 1971 British Lions halfway round the world for a series which was to change the course of world rugby . . . and was not to do the Mighty Mouse any harm either.

I never expected to tour. The Home Unions, acting wisely, had appointed the tour manager Doug Smith and the coach Carwyn James a year before, and soon afterwards I had a letter asking me if I was available, if selected. If you don't throw your cap in the ring, you'll never get anywhere, I thought, and promptly wrote back to say I would be delighted. But it was one thing to be on a short list, another thing to be selected – and what happened the night Scotland played France in Paris that year might have scuppered my chances.

After the match, I'd gone to a restaurant with my teammates Brian Simmers and Nairn McEwan, along with Norman Mair, a former Scottish cap, now the Rugby correspondent of the *Scotsman*. Norman insisted that he brought along another friend of his, a little Welshman who didn't say much and never stopped smoking. There was a lot of mickey-taking over who should pay the taxi, who should foot the bill – and I'm afraid the Scots rather ignored this other guy. Eventually, I asked Norman: 'Who the hell is this pal of yours?'

'Ian McLauchlan,' he replied, 'Meet Carwyn James.' It was an inauspicious first meeting with a character who, along with Bill Dickinson, stands head-and-shoulders above any other thinker on rugby I have ever met.

Anyway, after Scotland's last match of the season, another letter dropped through the letter-box of my home at Bishopbriggs, just outside Glasgow, and it contained a tour contract. I was to promise not to write a book on the tour within the next two years, give an undertaking that I would return straight home if injured, and there were details about the supply of slacks, blazers, that kind of thing. It must have taken me five seconds to sign it.

The next piece of business was to make sure I got leave of absence from Glasgow Corporation from my job as a PE teacher. I was going, you understand, but with Andrew just over two and wee Scott just a week old, I had to remember my family responsibilities. Oddly, the corporation never replied to my letter, but the money kept on coming while I was away. The bank manager said he would keep Eileen in funds, I picked up £150 in cash to top up my 75p-a-day expenses while on tour, and off I set – first to a week's pre-tour training at Eastbourne, then on to New Zealand.

Despite the fact that I was twenty-nine – and I'd gone on those Scottish tours of Argentina and Australia – I was very much a junior member of the Lions: a cub. But I was bursting to prove myself and the early weeks of that memorable tour were a disappointment to me. Ray McLoughlin of Ireland was the obvious first choice at loose head and as he was also pack leader my chances of making a Test team looked pretty slender. And Ray played in the opening match at Pukekohe against the Counties-Thames Valley which the Lions won comfortably 25–3. The two interesting points to emerge there were that the town itself – population 7000 – had a stadium holding 25,000 people, and that Barry John kicked sixteen points. It all proved that New Zealand was *the* rugby place but that King John was to be unstoppable the length and breadth of the South and North Islands.

I played my first match on the Wednesday in a win against Kings Country at Wanganui – my first sight of Colin Meads – and we won 22–9. But as we started to make the sweep across New Zealand I felt I wasn't getting too many chances. I was virtually the only member of the party not to get a Saturday game. This bothered me enough to raise the matter with Carwyn, who said that the sides were picked quite a lot in advance, that they were working up to the first test and that my chance would come. If you are going to be a good tourist and you respect the management you've just got to accept decisions like that, not go off in a huff and be a liability to everyone else. A doubly determined Ian MacLauchlan returned to training.

But Ray McLoughlin was in great form. Against Waitako, he was at his best and he told me afterwards: 'You won't believe it but I had to hold my opponent down just to have something to push against.' It was a pretty significant remark because it showed that the New Zealanders, who had never really bothered too much about scrummaging techniques – while at the same time being advanced in their understanding of the rucks and mauls – had a weakness which we could exploit. Still, it looked as if it would be Ray and not me who would do the exploiting.

The triumphant progress continued. I played against the Maoris when the 'King' got 20 of our 23 points but Ray was back again for the Wellington match, won by an incredible 47–9 (the 'King' got 19). After our first eight matches we were unbeaten, had scored 237 points and all of New Zealand were already admitting that we were the best Lions side of all time and some were even whispering that we might be the first British Isles team to go back as Test series winners. The alarm bells were ringing.

Our reputation, clearly, had gone ahead of us when we arrived at Canterbury for the last Saturday match before the first Test.

What happened is history of the worst kind. Mick Hipwell aggravated his cartilage injury, but at least that was an accident. Sandy Carmichael had both his eyes blacked and his right cheekbone shattered in five places and that wasn't an accident. Ray McLoughlin broke his thumb hitting Alex Wylie and Fergus Slattery took a punch in the mouth after only the third line-out and nearly lost all of his teeth.

I've never been one for trying to work out who started it.

These things happen. We had come to New Zealand knowing that the rugby would be physical and that previous Lions sides had been pushed around. We realized that we had to meet force – if it cropped up – with force. From where I sat in the stand, it wasn't too clear what was going on. Sandy was getting his doing from inside the scrum, presumably from the second row, but Sandy has always refused to say just from whom – and I respect his decision. Ray was unlucky. He mistimed his punch and jabbed his finger into Wylie's eye.

Canterbury had beaten the Lions in both '55 and '66 and were determined to do this lot. We were determined they wouldn't. Oddly, they might have gained that victory if they had played clean, because between the punch-ups they looked the best side we had met. John Bevan won the game for us, getting the ball and simply knocking guys over all the way to the line. The best try of pure physical agression I have ever seen. What I never want to see again is the sight of Sandy's face in the state it was that night.

We went back to the hotel, had a drink, and generally licked our wounds.

With the first Test just seven days away, it was the turning point of the tour. Sandy and Ray – our first choice props – were going home. The responsibility was now with my pal Sean Lynch and myself. We had a lot to play for – our own pride, our countries, the Lions and for Ray and Sandy. After a Tuesday win against Marlborough – Nelson Bay 31–12, we moved on to Dunedin where the All Blacks were waiting and our chances would come. 'BeJesus,' Sean would always splutter, usually in the middle of a maul when the going was tough. BeJesus, I thought to myself.


That Test is now history. What followed after we got back into the dressing rooms confirmed my belief that New Zealanders are my kind of people. The first visitor was Colin Meads, the All Blacks captain, who said: 'Now you've proved that you are the best Lions ever to come to our country.' He must have been pretty upset but it didn't show. It was the sportsmanship which mattered.

We went back to the Southern Cross Hotel where Sandy – soon to go home – was waiting for me. He said he'd had a heart attack when I scored and added maliciously: 'It must have been offside if you managed to get up to the ball.' Inside it was bedlam but we went into our private room for a celebration of our own. One supporter alone sent in £80-worth of champagne and that was a lot of money and a lot of champagne in those days. Left to ourselves we would probably have got brainless but we went off to the official function and that kept us vaguely in order for a few hours. Back at the hotel the party was in full swing and God only knows what time I got to bed that night. As Sean would have said about the entire day – and probably did – 'BeJesus.'

When we pulled ourselves together the next day and read all the papers, the significance of what we had done began to sink in. But there was to be no gloating, no relaxing, no resting on our laurels. As Willie John said to us: 'The show is now on the road.' The series now had to be won.

Tours are about fun. Nobody took the game more seriously than the 1971 Lions and I like to think that no British Lion took the game more seriously than I. McLauchlan (Jordanhill and Scotland). But it's the opportunity of a lifetime to make friends and see new places and you'd be mad if you didn't make the most of it. After all, you're not getting paid and it's not a job of work. On the field and in training it can be a desperately serious business because you don't want to let yourself or your teammates down. But it's a lot of laughs as well.

Like the time . . . we were a man short in scrummaging practice. So Bob Hiller – Hiller of the Harlequins – decided that he would make up the numbers and prop against me. Now when you are packing tight head, as he was, the loose head has his mouth right next to your ear. Just for a bit of fun, I decided to have a little nibble on his ear. Hiller of the Harlequins shot out of the scrum like a startled ferret. The next time J.P.R. Williams is chosen to pack against me. I nibbled at him. Next thing I know, I'm lying flat on my back because J.P.R.'s taken a swing at me and laid me out. He's into everything, J.P.R. – must like the pain.

Like the time . . . at Hudson Bay when Frankie Laidlaw is captain for the day and has to give the team talk in the dressing room. The way he's laying down the law, you'd think he was addressing the troops on the eve of Bannockburn. 'Think of your families; think of the boys back home,' he says. Sean Lynch and Mike Roberts burst out laughing. The next thing Frankie leaps across the dressing room and starts knocking hell out of them. And that's before the match.

Like the time . . . after the King County match. We were in the pub having a private party; Sandy and Dave Duckham are on the door trying to keep out the gatecrashers and they are taking some stick from the locals. 'Pommy Bastards!' they are shouting. Colin Meads is our guest and he tells us to leave it to him. Pine Tree goes to the door and looks down on them, then says: 'These people are personal friends of mine. If you abuse them I take it as a personal insult . . . and you know what that means.' You've never seen a crowd disperse so quickly in your life.

Like the time . . . Barry John and Ray McLoughlin are talking about their own personal philosophies on the game. That's a laugh for a start. Ray's talking about scrums, about knocking people over, taking them out of rucks. Barry is nattering on about flip passing, diagonal kicking, watching wing-forwards' feet. Barry says to Ray: 'We're not talking about the same game. In fact I don't think we are playing the same game.'

There followed a string of Irish expletives and Ray says, 'No, my game's a better game.'

'Ah well,' says Barry. 'Next season when Wales play Ireland, I'll certainly be in the Welsh side. Maybe you'll get a game for Ireland: they're always short of men. And if you get within ten yards of me, I'll hang up my boots. I'll know it's time to retire.'

That brought the house down and even Delme Thomas had to admit the truth about the Welsh training sessions at Porthcawl; they play touch rugby. They give the ball to Barry and the other twenty-nine try to touch him. And that was the same Barry we saw on that tour. Untouchable.

Like the time . . . in Nelson, where there was a beer strike. They should have declared a state of national emergency but we took matters into our own hands and 'acquired' a few cases from the Banquet on the Saturday night, running up the fire escapes with them and hiding the cans in our rooms. On a Sunday, John Dawes led a clique known as the Sunday School, the gin-drinking set. This Sunday they fancied a beer but couldn't get one, so we started flaunting the stuff in front of them. I was a member of the Front Row Union, their deadliest enemies. When J.P.R. realized we weren't joking, that they were not going to get any beer from us, he wanted to take on the world. A frightening man, J.P.R.

Like the time . . . Bob Hiller was asked by a very posh guy at one of the receptions, 'How do you find New Zealand?'

'Easy,' replied Bob: 'You just go to the end of the world and it's lying there.'


We hit our bad patch of the tour after the First Test and should have lost our unbeaten record against Taranaki who didn't even rate themselves. They pushed us hard and we were lucky to emerge unscathed 14–9, thanks largely to Bob Hiller's boot. The trouble was that a touch of overconfidence had spread through the squad and we were beginning to believe that anybody could be beaten without too much trouble. That attitude is fatal at all times – and it persisted until the Second Test at Christchurch.

We lost it, 22–12. To be honest we had become obsessed by scrummaging at the expense of other parts of our game, like fringe defence. We had pushed the All Blacks at will in Dunedin, feeling that this was the area of our game we had to get right. We forgot that the other things don't follow on automatically. So, in the Second Test Sid Going was able to score a try himself going down the blindside. Sid had a hand in four of the five New Zealand tries and generally had the game of his life. The All Blacks also scored the try of the series when Ian Kirkpatrick pulled a ball out of a ruck on the half-way line, peeled away and then outpaced everyone to the corner flag, handing off Gareth and J.P.R. along the way – no mean feat.

The talking point of the Test was the penalty try awarded to the All Blacks after an early tackle by Gerald on Bryan Williams, a close decision but a fair one because referee Pring had a fine series. We only found our best form near the end of the game when it was too late.

It was the crossroads of the tour. But curiously we were not too downhearted. I was just one of many players who felt that we had played better in Christchurch than we had in Dunedin. The general consensus was that we had been a wee bit lucky in the First Test and not got the breaks in the Second. We had won the first match with only 30 per cent of the ball and relied on Barry to torment the New Zealanders to death. When we lost, it was because the All Blacks capitalized on our own slack play rather than that they created too much for themselves.

In short the defeat knocked all the complacency out of us but didn't damage our overall belief that we were the better side. It stopped a downhill slide in attitude which had become apparent. If we were to lose a Test, this was the one. It gave us time to come back and try and win the series. No one doubted we could still do it.

We had formed our own little group, the Front Row Union. Membership was strictly limited – myself, Sean Lynch, Mike Roberts, Frank Laidlaw, John Pullin and, when he arrived, Stack Stevens. There was one honorary member, Arthur Lewis, who joined us, I suspect, because he didn't fancy the gin-and-tonic set from the London Welsh. Arthur must have been one of the great tourists of all time. If we were feeling down, if we were moaning about anything, Arthur would pipe up, smiles all over his face: 'Better than being at home in the steelworks.'

After the Second Test we all flew up to Whangaray in an old Fokker Friendship, right through a tropical storm at 200 feet, for a few days' rest. Or that's what we thought as the party started in the hotel: but we really got stuck in amongst the grog and Stack threw a pint of beer right over this guy in a white suit at the dance. Carwyn saw it all and just came across to say quietly, 'Training will be hard tomorrow lads.' And so it was. The most hilarious part of it came when the threequarters were all sent off on a cross country run. Barry John was less than amused by the thought and soon fell right behind all the others. They plodded on for a few miles wondering where Barry was when suddenly a lorry carrying oranges passed them on the road. There was Barry peering out of the driver's cab and giving the others a wave.

I mention these two Welshmen together because they were the most important Lions. As a coach Carwyn had it all put together. One of his ploys was to invite three or four players to his room for a drink and then have dinner together. This was an invitation no one would refuse, not just because it was more of a royal command, but because, as well as being the supreme coach, Carwyn was also a very good judge of a bottle of wine. At the first of these little get-togethers, I thought he was taking the mickey because he seemed to ask questions about the scrum which were blindingly obvious: 'He's playing the schoolmaster, making me pass a test,' was my conclusion. Then I realized that he was putting out feelers to see the way you thought about things.

What impressed me about him as a man was that he didn't care who got the credit for our success. Always he used the royal 'we'. But his feel for the game was unrivalled and he was a great handler of men. Maybe his biggest quality was spotting when someone had gone over the top and needed a rest. Quietly he would say to them, 'Have a break tomorrow.' And the other players didn't start moaning because they were training while a teammate had the day off. They knew it was Carwyn unobtrusively at work.

Which brings me on to Barry. Barry would train hard when he felt like it and if he didn't then nothing and no one could get him to stir himself. But the 'King' always produced the goods when they were needed. Oddly enough it was only when I played against him later that I realized just how brilliant he was. There had been a moment in the First Test when Alan McNaughton, the All Blacks breakaway, had tackled him so late that it might have been a week last Friday. McNaughton wasn't that kind of player. It must have been sheer bloody frustration and I can understand why.

Later on in the tour we played a very brutal match against Hawkes Bay. The trouble started in the first scrum which ended up with a fullscale punch-up and tempers were lost again after John Pullin had been punched and carried off. Now Barry doesn't like this sort of thing at all. Like any great artist, it offends his sense of style as much as anything else. So near the end, he gathered the ball and waited for the wing-forward to come at him. Then he showed him the ball with one hand, pulled it around his back and showed it to him again with the other. This guy, of course, slips over and is on his knees. White with temper. Barry gives him a withering glance, then pats him on the head and kicks the ball into touch. Strictly speaking, it was a bit of a provocative act and I wouldn't like to see any young player behave that way. But coming from the 'King' it seemed right. I asked him after-wards why he did it and Barry replied it was his way of humiliating them, of proving the game was never meant to be played the way the New Zealanders were playing it that afternoon.

The Third Test was probably won and lost before a ball was kicked. The New Zealand Rugby Union had given us the week off, so to speak. There was no Wednesday game and so we retreated to work out our battle plans undisturbed. As usual, Carwyn had no doubts about where we needed to tighten up – in our back row defence. There had been a moment in the Second Test when we were pushing the All Blacks scrum back about five yards but still Going managed to pick up the ball, streak past the flankers and set up an attack. So Sid Going, along with Ian Kirkpatrick, working round the edges of the New Zealand scrum, was the man who we concerned ourselves with.

Carwyn picked Derek Quinnell and Fergus Slattery as the men for the job and in all our training sessions Chico Hopkins did an impersonation of Going as we worked out our tactics. As it turned out Slatts had to miss the game because of 'flu but with John Taylor knowing full well what was required of him, that didn't make too much difference.

It was the All Blacks who got themselves into a pre-match mess. All week, they had been perturbed by an ankle injury which was bothering Colin Meads. That cleared up only for them to face another body blow when the other lock Peter Whiting went down with stabbing pains during the Thursday training session. The next day it was no better and we were enjoying the All Blacks' discomfiture as we read about it in the papers and heard it on TV. They had twenty-eight hours to replace a vital man. They decided to recall that splendid forward Brian Lochore but it was a mistake. The Lions went into the Test settled and determined, while the New Zealanders were still wondering whether they had done the right thing after Whiting's call-off.

We had another bit off luck in winning the toss and being able to use a fairly considerable wind. Carwyn felt that we needed early points and he wasn't let down. After eighteen minutes we had scored 13 points and that period settled the match and the series. A quick drop goal by Barry gave us the fillip we needed and then Gerald took a quick pass from Gareth to touch down in the corner. Predictably, Barry's conversion went over after hitting the upright and we were firmly in charge.

The 'King' wasn't finished. He ended a fine Gareth break with a try beside the post, converted it himself and had personally scored 10 points as, to all intents and purposes we had the match won. We'd already called him the 'King'. I think we would have made him God at that moment. After that, we got all the possession we needed and made fairly good use of it, but it was clear that the All Blacks weren't going to come back and we coasted the rest of the way. That night the beer flowed, the songs were sung and we were already assured of at least sharing the series – something that no British side had done – and we were confident of winning it.

The problem with any last Test is that everyone has one foot on the plane. You suddenly realize how much you have missed the wife and children. If you're not the best-organized person – and I'm not always – then you remember that you should take home a few presents. But that's not all. The last match of any tour becomes a bit of a reunion of all the people you've met along the way. They turn up, they take you out shopping, they buy you a drink. That all has the effect of taking your mind off the business at hand – winning.

I remember a couple of days before that last match someone coming back to the hotel and telling us that there was a super shop a couple of blocks away which sold Maori woodcarvings. You could see the fellows saying to themselves, 'Just the thing for presents,' and there was a mass exodus to do the last-minute gift-buying. It was the same in South Africa. In fact it's been the same on every tour. In New Zealand, the hospitality being what it is, rugby can suddenly become the last thing on your mind.

Then there was a disturbance in the hotel on Friday night. Looking back it was quite funny, although we didn't see it that way then. Some New Zealand guy managed to get up to our corridor in the middle of the night and started banging on our doors to disturb us.

The trouble – for him – was that when he was halfway along the corridor two doors opened and he saw Willie John and Delme Thomas blocking his way out. That's the moment when he probably thought how it might be more comfortable to face the firing squad. Anyway, he took the least line of resistance, hurtled towards the fire escape, jumped down the last flight of stairs and was gone. That kind of quick thinking at least kept him alive.

As I said, concentration was difficult and the Test was upon us almost before we realized. The All Blacks had to salvage something in front of a 56,000 crowd with black market tickets changing hands at thirty dollars a time. Quickly we were eight points down and we wondered whether it would be a Wellington in reverse. But New Zealand couldn't add to that and when Barry kicked his first penalty we were back in the match with a vengeance. We were level just before half-time when Peter Dixon scored a try from a line-out and the 'King' did the rest. The New Zealanders had seen their lead evaporate and when Barry kicked another penalty we were ahead. Then the remarkable J.P.R. succeeded with a superb dropped goal and we led again 14–11. True, the All Blacks pulled us back with a

Laurie Mains penalty to make it 14–14. But the draw was as good as a win because it gave us the series . . . and the historic honour of being the first Lions ever to beat the All Blacks.

I had gone to New Zealand as second choice and was going home as a man amongst men. Gradually it sunk in on us that we had changed the face of world rugby – and set up, for the Seventies, the game's most exciting period. I had made friends amongst the New Zealanders and the Lions. That was the best reward of all. I remembered the presents – just.

# 8

# Welsh Wales

I wouldn't have minded being a Welshman. Coming from a mining village in Ayrshire, with a father who knew first-hand the dangers of going underground, I've always felt myself a brother under the skin to people in the Principality. I'd have loved to have played a part of my career in Wales.

To play at the National Stadium in Cardiff is the great experience of anyone's life. If I have a regret, it's the fact that I've never played in a winning Scotland side there. Much as I love them, it would have done the Welsh no harm to be reminded that there are a few people about outside their country who know how the game should be played. Off the field I liked them. On the field I hated them. That's how it should be.

Rugby to the Welsh is what football is to the Scots. It's not just a game, it's more a way of life. The country's whole virility seems to be judged on the way the team is performing. When Wales win a Triple Crown, I imagine the production figures up and down the Rhondda Valleys shoot up, just as they do in Glasgow when Scotland qualifies for a World Cup.

To take on Wales at Cardiff is to take on the whole Welsh nation. You are not just dealing with a side which throughout the Seventies was far and away the best in the world. You are also taking on 50,000 fervent Welshmen in the stands and everyone watching in the towns and villages along the greatest stretch of rugby country anywhere. If you get caught at the bottom of a ruck, you feel it is all those countless thousands who are lying on top of you. If you drive into a tackle, you feel you have to knock down the same number of people.

Yet Wales – and Cardiff on international days – is one of

68

the friendliest places too. I suppose you will find a few Welshmen who, just because they are Welsh, think that they know all about rugby and that anyone else is inferior. I met a handful of Welsh players who felt the same way. But the vast majority of Welshmen are neither obnoxious nor arrogant despite their success. I wonder if the same could be said of the Scots if they *did* win the World Cup.

To go to Wales is to go to the home of rugby. It never ceases to amaze me when, on the morning of a match, Welshmen come up to you and simply ask if you mind standing there while friends take a photograph. And you don't get the kind of patter you might elsewhere. They are not sidling up to you and muttering that you're about to get a good doing that afternoon. They are genuinely humble about it all. They just want a snapshot to take home with them. The craziest request I ever had was from a fellow who wanted to take my footprints in concrete so that he could hang them up in a restaurant he was building. How can you refuse something like that?

The Welsh understand rugby. So they should. They are weaned on it from the cradle onwards. They will be passing a ball about before they go to school They will be watching games as lads. And they enter into a highly structured system of rugby which ensures that talent is well looked after – and that success will follow automatically. I just wish the same could be said about Scotland.

I'd rather play ten games at Cardiff than one at Twickenham, where I find that hostility really exists. At Twickenham, you get this feeling of remoteness. On the field there is a highly competitive game of football going on but it rarely communicates itself to the spectators. There are far too many of the 'Ra Ra' brigade who are only at the match because it's an occasion, a chance to show off and munch the chicken legs and wash down the wine in the car parks before and after.

In Cardiff, from the moment you arrive for an international on the Thursday, you are aware of a great happening about to take place. The talk buzzes about rugby non-stop – and it's good, well-informed talk. The secret is, I think that just about every able-bodied Welshman can think of no greater privilege or honour in life than to pull the famous red jersey over his head and represent his country. That makes Wales unique, certainly inside Great Britain. On a very personal note, every other person in Wales appears to recognize me. That's more than can be said even in Edinburgh where I live. I don't mind that recognition at all.

They have it organized in Wales. I don't think there is any great quality about Welshmen as such which makes them natural rugby players. Their love of the game ensures that there is a constant interest in it – and then the Welsh Rugby Union, by and large, makes sure that everything is done correctly. The little clubs feed the bigger clubs and beneath that level there is well-run rugby for youngsters and teenagers. Because there aren't too many top clubs, it means that potential Welsh caps are under constant inspection by the selectors – and they are playing pressure football all the time. And it's pressure which makes a player. The matches between Cardiff, Newport, Llanelli, Pontypool, Aberavon, Bridgend and their likes are all absolutely top-class games between world-famous clubs. The competition is intense and the standard high. It's no wonder that they keep on throwing up good Welsh sides because nothing succeeds like success.

There are as many different types of Welshmen as there are Scots. There are the quiet home-loving ones like Delme Thomas, the up-and-down guy like Chico Hopkins who, like most scrum-halves could be on cloud nine and the joker one minute, but in the depths of despair the next. There are the elegant, eloquent ones, of whom Barry John is the best example, a 'King' who knew exactly how to wear his crown. Then there's Gareth who had to be into everything, and John Taylor, who seemed so quiet but who was the leader of the choir and knew the words to every tune. There's J.P.R., and I've heard people say he's arrogant. Not a bit of it. He has the confidence of a man who knows that he's the best fullback there's ever been in the game. There's Arthur Lewis, whose smile would melt an iceberg and then, last but not least, there is the Pontypool front row.

Of all the Welsh friends I ever made I've got to single out Bobby 'the Duke' Windsor. There's no one more ordinary and down-to-earth – in the best sense – than Bobby. Once we were out shooting springbok on a game reserve in South Africa. At the end of the day our host counted up the haul: 'You got fifteen,' he told us. 'Got the whole side then, didn't we?' said Bobby. They counted again and found that we had bagged sixteen. 'Got the referee as well. Mind you, he bloody deserved it,' Bobby quipped.

What they had was a great passion for the game. It's often said that Welshmen don't make good tourists and like most clichés it's mostly wrong but with an element of truth. Welshmen seem to suffer from homesickness more than any-body else. That was true in New Zealand in 1971 when one or two of them moped about, constantly talking of their home and their families. But if you are going to have a fault, then I can't think of a better one. And never, never did they let it worry them on the pitch.

In 1972, we were in Cardiff, and both Scotland and Wales were staying in the Angel Hotel. It's not easy to ignore guys with whom you spent the previous summer touring on the other side of the world. On the Friday night Derek Quinnell and I had quite a blether. He had been on a Lions tour but was still waiting for his first Welsh cap. The next morning, we bumped into each other in the lobby and he said: 'McLauch-lan, this is the last time I will speak to you until this evening. But you have my permission to assassinate any of the Welsh back five.' When Derek eventually did get his first cap – as a replacement – there was one of the greatest television pictures of all time: him running down the tunnel, charging policemen out of the way and just bursting to get on to the field in that red jersey. It summed up to me everything that is good about Welsh rugby and its meaning to people in that country.

But I would have liked, just once, to have won in Wales and given them a bit of a doing in their own backyard. My first visit, in 1970, was inauspicious, to say the least. We went down to stay in a hotel in Penarth, now mercifully closed down. It was like a rough-and-tumble boarding house, a disaster. On the Friday night we all went to bed early and Sandy Carmichael, with whom I was sharing a room, was fast asleep when a hoo-ha started next door. It was some members of the SRU committee who had decided they would have an impromptu party. We were through there like a shot telling them, in no uncertain fashion, what we thought about the noise. I didn't mince my words, then as ever. The match, on a mudheap, was nothing special; Scotland were beaten 18–9 and the aftermath was that I was dropped for the next game, even though we were up in the scrums and strikes against the head. I sought out a selector to ask why I had been made the scapegoat.

'We didn't win enough good ruck ball,' he replied.

I wondered how he could expect props to win good ruck ball if it wasn't properly set up for them. Anyway I was out after what must have been the most novel excuse of all time by a selector explaining a dropping.

The score, two years later, looks bad: 35–12. But honestly, it wasn't as calamitous as that. Scotland were actually leading at half-time and who knows what might have happened if P.C. hadn't decided to take a quick line-out which John Taylor intercepted and ran in for a try. Once in front, Wales, with the choirs singing, ran in the tries but there had been glimpses of what was to come. From 1973 to 1975 we more than held our own.

At Murrayfield in '73 I was captain of Scotland for the first time. Previously the set-up had been ambiguous with P.C. as a skipper and myself leading the pack. That doesn't make sense to me. If you are a captain and a forward, then you should lead the pack as well as the team. It was the greatest honour so far in my career.

I see no difficulty in a prop being captain. The job is more about the type of person you are than about the position in which you play. A captain, too, depends a lot on the people he is asked to skipper. I've seen a lot of supposedly 'great' captains go down when the team has gone down collectively. Take Jean Pierre Rives who was hailed as the greatest French skipper of all when his side drew a Test series in New Zealand for the first time ever. Then a year later, before France squeezed home against Ireland, he was facing the guillotine. What I am saying is that there is only so much a player can do on the field as skipper.

Beforehand is a different matter. It's the captain's job to

make sure the team sticks together, that the spirit is good and – in conjunction with the coach – to ensure that the preparation and planning are thoroughly implemented. But your success or otherwise as captain largely depends on how the other fourteen are playing.

The decisions which can give rise to difficulty mostly involve the kicks at goal. In 1975, when we were playing England for the Triple Crown, I had to decide whether to let Dougie Morgan or Andy Irvine take the kicks. Now that's not easy because they are both fine kickers of a ball: they can both heft it over from long range and from both sides of the field.

I decided on Dougie simply because I thought he was the more consistent of the two – and then he went and missed them. But you have to back your own judgement and I would do exactly the same thing again. We usually decided who was first choice beforehand and stuck with it – which is nerve-wracking in the sense that Andy is likely to miss a couple and then put over the third – much harder – shot.

Anyway, I was vastly helped in my first match by the man I replaced, P.C. He was still in the team and no one could have been of more assistance both before the match and in it where he won a lot of good line-out ball.

We did everything right to beat Wales that year. In the Sunday session before the match Bill Dickinson concentrated on the forward play. We were shifting a lot of tonnage at that period and the scrumming machine took a terrible pounding. We pushed it from the Murrayfield Ice Rink to the railway embankment and back again. If Dickie had told us to push it up that embankment and on to the line, we'd have done that as well. We had a fair conceit of ourselves after that effort.

Our tactical plan was quite simple and we had that worked out as well. We knew that Wales would play overlap rugby. J.P.R. would come up into the line, drag our cover in and help produce the good ball. That was their style and we didn't see that they had much reason to alter it. All we had to do was to make sure it didn't work.

That left the team talk. 'I wish I had been a fly on the wall listening to what McLauchlan said about us,' Gerald Davies remarked afterwards. Well, here's exactly what I did say: 'The Welsh think we are a load of scrubbers. Just think who's in that dressing room over there – people like J.P.R., Bennett, Gareth, etc. They have about a dozen British Lions in there. And they think we'll be easy meat, don't they. I know I would if I were Welsh. Well, we're not easy meat, we're not second-raters. If they think we have no chance, let them. But I think we've got a great chance of winning. Just as long as we get wired into them straight away – and keep it up for eighty minutes.'

And that's what we did. All the Scottish scoring came in the first twenty minutes. Billy Steele got a try and then Colin Telfer another. That one I remember as if it were yesterday. He broke left, spotted a gap, went through it and ran on for the touchdown. It was the first time I ever noticed that Colin actually could accelerate. Lots of people claim it was the first and last time that Colin did accelerate. With a Dougie Morgan conversion, we were 10 points up and with Colin playing well we weren't in too much danger for the rest of the game. Colin was my kind of fly-half. As long as he could keep the forwards going forward he knew that the game was ours and that's the way it turned out to be.

We had been to war and we had won. We were out of our minds with it that night and I always remember smiling with satisfaction as Arthur Lewis got up to make his speech as Welsh captain. 'This is a unique occasion. I have never made a speech as losing captain before,' he said. More than that, we had stopped Wales from scoring a try, a feat in itself. The Triple Crown bid went wrong later that season – but it was a match to savour then, and it still is.

To my dying day I will claim that we were diddled in 1974. Wales won 6–0 with a try that should never have been. It came after one of the great covering tackles of all time by Nairn McEwan on Gerald Davies. I'm sure Gerald fell on the ball, but, the wizard that he is, he managed to flip it up and Wales scored. True Scotland didn't score themselves but we knew that we had given them a drubbing; we gained all the possession we wanted and needed but somehow didn't convert that into points. I know that was a common Scottish failing at that period but when did you last hear a Cardiff crowd whistling desperately for the final whistle as they did that day? They knew how lucky their side had been. It was the nearest I ever came to winning in Wales and we all took it hard. To add insult to injury, poor Nairn never got a place in the Lions touring party for South Africa that summer. He deserved it all round.

The 1975 match between Scotland and Wales at Murrayfield must go down as one of the most amazing occasions that ground has ever seen. Oddly, I had been talking to one of the SRU committee men just beforehand and said to him – only half jokingly: 'You know, we haven't been beaten on our ground for four years or so. If this keeps on, then you'll have the perfect opportunity to double the prices and make a fortune.'

'Oh,' he said, 'I don't think a winning team makes much difference to the crowd.'

That bright afternoon, there was an estimated 104,000 inside Murrayfield with thousands locked out. Many disappointed Welshmen who had travelled up to stay in places as far apart as Greenock, Perth and even Carlisle, never got in. The terraces bulged. Afterwards the SRU admitted 'Obviously the spread of the game, allied to a successful Scottish side, has brought many more spectators to Murrayfield. The Union will give consideration to the advisability of making certain future games all-ticket.'

In a word, I was right.

The flags obscured almost all those spectators and they weren't by any means all Scottish. The Welsh were there in their masses, having taken over Princes Street all morning. Long may they continue to come and enjoy our Scottish hospitality, even if they find tickets hard to get.

We could hardly fail in that atmosphere and didn't. My team talk was similar to that which I had given two years before: 'Remember, it's war.' And I added for good measure that Wales were the luckiest so-and-so's in the world to have beaten us in Cardiff twelve months before. The Triple Crown was beckoning tantalisingly again. That pack, as mature now as good Dunlop cheese, did the rest of the work and pushed the Welsh about. Dougie Morgan gave us the lead with a penalty after Mervyn Davies had been penalized for climbing up an opponent at the back of the line-out. Steve Fenwick equalized, Dougie thumped over another and again Fenwick levelled it. Before half-time Dougie had put his third kick over and later, when Ian McGeechan dropped a lovely goal, we looked safe with a 12–6 lead.

But then Gerald produced one of his magical moments with a little inside run that caught out Andy Irvine and David Bell. His pass gave Trevor Evans the chance to make a dash for the corner which Al McHarg tried to stop – but couldn't. So, deep in injury time, it all hinged on Alan Martin's conversion. I remember how John Taylor had robbed us four years before and held my breath. He missed. We relaxed – and seconds later there were thousands swarming all over the field.

It was Dougie's day in more ways than one. Ten minutes before the end, the McLauchlan legs were beginning to get a bit rubbery. 'How long to go?' I said to him. 'Never you mind, just keep on running,' he replied. That, from the novice to the captain, was the first indication of just what a warrior the little scrum-half was – and is. Later that night the North British was mobbed by Welsh supporters and it was pleasant to walk through them to the banquet knowing that they had all received exactly what we wanted them to have – a very pleasant visit to Scotland, a good few pints – and a defeat.

Of 1976's 28–6 defeat by Wales in Cardiff, enough said. It was a drubbing.

I was back the next year as we went for three in a row against the Welsh at Murrayfield, but only just. Sandy and I had lost our places against the Japanese at the start of the season with Norman Pender and Jim Aitken coming in as the props elect. I think my captaincy had been weighing on the selectors' minds. I had beaten the record and they seemed to be saying 'Enough is enough.' For the first time I was listed as a veteran. Maybe I should have seen it coming when I was left out but frankly didn't. I was still the best Scottish loose head – at least in my opinion. I was determined to get back in the team with another tour to New Zealand coming up. After a 26–6 defeat at Twickenham, the selectors had second thoughts and I was back in the team, determined to run my guts out to make sure I was on that plane.

I was going to prove the resurrection of the dead.

The match will always be remembered for the Phil Bennett try which finished us off and took Wales to an 18–9 win. But I came within inches of stopping him.

It all started with an Andy Irvine chip through to J.P.R., not the cleverest of moves. But luckily Sandy, back as well, went at the fullback like a steamroller and when Sandy comes at you, he doesn't miss. Any lesser player than J.P.R. would have been counting stars and not too worried about where the ball had gone but he managed, incredibly, to flip it up. Wales continued the move in a way which tells you everything about their rugby, always having enough men about to launch attacks from improbable positions and then showing all kinds of different skills to get them across the line. Gerald kept the attack going and slipped the ball to Phil, who jinked through to fall flat on his face under the posts, clutching the ball like a man who knows that the try will be shown for as long as rugby is played as one of the great ones. It certainly was.

But I might just have stopped it after a marathon run, sweeping towards the touchline and then running back to try and get at Phil. As I say, I was bursting my guts out that day. Unfortunately Bill Gammell came across and got in my way a bit, just as I was about to make a despairing dive at the fly-half. If Bill had stayed with J.J. Williams who was up in support, I might have caught Phil by surprise for the tackle of the century.

It was a great Welsh side and a good win. Scotland were too predictable and Wales did what they are so good at . . . sitting back, mopping up the pressure and then hitting you hard. The try was a beauty. But the important point was that the Scottish pack hadn't come out of the game badly. I thought there was a chance that I could be going back to New Zealand.

It soon became obvious at the after-match banquet that I wasn't. John Dawes, who had been appointed Lions coach, was there and he made it perfectly clear that he didn't want to know McLauchlan. That was his mistake.

The Scottish lads were sitting around and Dawes was standing at the bar having a drink. Sandy went across to say hello and have a bit of a chat about the old times but instead the Welsh coach went to have a word with J.P.R. He didn't even speak to me all evening and when I went home that night I knew I wasn't going to New Zealand. We never spoke a word to each other.

Of the eight Scottish forwards who played that day, not one went on the Lions tour. Of the eight Welshmen, seven did. And there wasn't much, if anything between the packs. Jim Renwick, who was the best centre-threequarter in Britain by a mile, wasn't picked and in the end nineteen of the touring party were Welsh. Work that one out.

It was clear to me that John Dawes wanted the 1977 tour to be John Dawes' tour. In 1971, and on the 1974 tour to South Africa, touring players had passed on the knowledge they gained in one trip to the newcomers on another. That didn't happen in 1977.

Watched from afar it clearly turned out to be a disaster. In 1971 we had won a series with fifty per cent of possession against the All Blacks. Six years later the Lions got far more ball and lost. Something must have been very wrong somewhere. Lack of leadership could be the answer.

That soured the 1977 Welsh match in retrospect – and three more straight defeats at their hands shows that the Scots had fallen back since that fine side in the early and middle Seventies. Meanwhile the Welsh roll on with good new players arriving on that conveyor belt which takes them into a winning side, and keeps them at the top – or very near it. As I said, they are generally the best. I'd just have loved to have beaten them in Cardiff. And then, if I really was resurrected, I'd promise to come back as a Welshman. Even learn to sing.

I'll never quite forgive John Taylor for what he did in the 1971 match. We certainly thought we had done enough to win until we were robbed in the last seconds when John popped over a conversion from the touch line and Wales beat us by the narrowest margin of all: 19–18. This was Bill Dickinson's first match as coach and I had more reasons than the rest of the side for hoping that Bill would get off to a win.

Seven times the lead changed hands as Murrayfield was in a constant uproar. Under Bill's guidance the Mean Machine moved into top gear and even Clive Rowlands thought that we had had the better of that part of the match.

With ten minutes left we were leading 18–14, thanks to a super Chris Rea try. P.C.'s conversion attempt cannoned off the post. If it had gone over Wales would have needed two scores to win the match and that would have been beyond them. As it was, they managed to come back again when Gerald Davies outpaced our defence to bring them back to within a single point. It all rested on John's final kick. Murrayfield held its breath and I held mine. I was praying inwardly that he would miss it but instead it flew straight between the posts and suddenly there seemed to be about 30,000 red scarves all being thrown in the air. I looked at Sandy and Gordon, P.C., Rodger Arneill and Nairn McEwan and saw complete and utter despondency written all over their faces. It was not to be. But at least Dickie, who had only just been appointed, had made an immediate improvement to the planning and morale of the Scottish side and better days were just around the corner. But we didn't think that way as we cried into our beer and wondered just what we had to do to beat that formidable Welsh side.

# 9
# South Africa 1974

Sitting in my bedroom in the Llandrost Hotel at the end of the British Lions 1974 tour to South Africa, I at last had a chance to catch up with the mail which had been accumulating over the weeks. There were many invitations I had been unable to accept, invitations asking me to talk or just visit people in this most hospitable of all countries. There were notes of thanks. And there was a little letter which simply said: 'Go home – and don't come back. We don't want your sort in our country. You are not welcome.'

It was obviously the work of a crank and it wasn't typical of the friendship which we had found all over South Africa, but it was a postscript to what the Lions had achieved in the previous months. For once, the statistics tell most of the story. We had won twenty-two matches and drawn the other. We had won the Test series 3–0 with one drawn. We had scored 729 points against 208. It was the most successful Lions tour of this century.

Since then, I wish I had been given a quid every time someone came up to me in a clubhouse and asked: 'How do you compare the Lions of 1971 in New Zealand with the 1974 side?' I could have retired by now. To me, there was no comparison. The Lions in South Africa were far and away the better team.

For a start, the pack was in a different class and the nice thing about it was that it contained two Englishmen, two Scots, two Welshmen and two Irish. Without any false modesty, I'd go so far as to say that it was the best Lions pack of all time. Behind it Gareth Edwards was a King, playing the best rugby of his life, far better than the slightly hesitant stuff he had produced three years before. For weeks on end, no South African side managed a try against our Saturday side and much of the credit there must go to Dick Milliken and Ian McGeechan. They became great personal friends and have stayed that way. There wasn't anything they wouldn't do for each other and that showed.

If you add players like Billy Steele, Andy Irvine and J.J. Williams on the wing, all ready, even desperate, to run in tries, it all adds up to a pretty formidable combination. And on top of that lot there was always J.P.R., rock solid at fullback.

Like 1971, the success of the tour was based not just on the Test team, which pretty early on began to pick itself, but on the attributes of the other members of the party. Take John Moloney. It was obvious that unless Gareth got injured, his chances of getting the first team spot at scrum-half were non-existent. He could have been excused if he had just gone for the joy ride but I don't remember anyone training harder – a real 110 percenter.

Another story sums up the spirit. Before the match against Transvaal in Jo'burg, Sandy Carmichael, Tommy Grace, J.P.R., Bobby Windsor, Ian McGeechan and myself all went down with a bad bout of 'flu. Ken Kennedy, who's a doctor, looked after us all. You couldn't have blamed Ken if he had taken the attitude that he was here as a rugby player and not as a doctor and left it to someone else. But he tended us night and day, hardly getting a wink of sleep for forty-eight hours. The result was that all of us, apart from Geechs, played in that match and we won.

All throughout that tour, Micky Burton was suffering from an injured knee. He really could have been sent home at any time and probably would have been if Ken hadn't worked out a separate training programme for him, went through it with him every day and nursed him through the trip.

It was the sort of commitment you need in South Africa because it's a far more difficult place in which to win than New Zealand. They breed really big boys, bigger even than the All Blacks. And it was a violent tour. But you could reel off the names of our crowd who just weren't going to be messed about – Bobby Windsor, Fran Cotton, Willie John McBride, Tony Nearey, Chris Ralston, Mervyn Davies, Mike Burton, Gordon Brown and, as always, J.P.R. I'd better put my own name in that list as well.

In South Africa, they don't make a big hoo-hah about the rough stuff. The papers don't keep going on about it. It's just part of the way they play the game. So it's advisable, if you want to succeed, to be in there swinging yourself.

In a good touring side, it can become second nature. In any game, anywhere, it can be physical. Even though 99.9 per cent of the contact is inadvertent. If a fifteen stone guy stands on top of you wearing aluminium studs, you are going to get badly mangled unless you have skin like a crocodile. You accept it – then forget about it. But on tour you are eating, drinking, sleeping rugby for three months, so you form a brotherhood and you are interested in protecting each other as well as looking after yourself. That's what happened on that trip.

It had its funny moments. The Lions in 1971 had invented this code '99'. If that was shouted you just waded into whichever All Black happened to be nearest to you. Retaliate first was the motto. We had to use it occasionally in South Africa, but in one match, the opposition had the throw at the line-out and this guy shouts '99' as he throws. It turned out later that it was an entirely different shout to tell his jumpers where he was putting the ball. Of course, we didn't know that and everyone was diving in. Apart from McLauchlan, who reacted a bit too slowly and caught the ball. So I was standing there with the ball watching this incredible punch-up going on all around me. Even the South Africans had a good laugh about it later.

It all meant we were a pretty hard bunch. And any South African who thought he could make a name for himself by laying out a Lion soon discovered differently. Definitely, this was a better side than in New Zealand.

I knew that I would enjoy the tour. Before the 1971 trip, I had only been abroad the twice, to Argentina with Scotland, which was interesting and to Australia with Scotland, which was a shambles. So, three years before, I felt a bit overawed

and still a novice. I'd been lucky in New Zealand getting a·
Test place which probably wasn't there before we started out.
This time, I had been mentioned as a possible captain and
realized that, unless my form went completely to pieces, I was
first choice. Being a senior member gave me a lot of confidence
and I revelled in the responsibility that the management gave
me.

I nearly went on tour as a frozen meat salesman. Applying
for leave of absence had led to a furore in the Edinburgh
corporation and Ian McLauchlan was a political pawn in the
debate over apartheid. Labour members of the council were
opposed to my request being granted. It was a dirty battle and
I didn't want to be drawn into it. But I desperately wanted to
go there and play rugby. As the debate went on, I had a lot of
letters delivered to my home and to Murrayfield, urging me
not to go. Equally, I had a lot of letters urging me to tour.
What the politicians don't realize is that being selected for a
tour is an honour in itself and the chance to spend three
months playing rugby comes to any player once – or if you are
lucky – twice in a lifetime. It's easy for politicians, who jet
about the world, to ask others to make a decision based on
their own conscience, but it's not so easy when your big
chance arrives.

Anyway, this guy turns up on the doorstep one night and
advises me to quit teaching and work for him selling frozen
meat. He will pay me during the time I'm on tour and then I'll
start work for him afterwards. It was a kind offer, but in the
end I didn't have to decide because my leave of absence was
granted, and I set off.

We all checked into the Britannia Hotel in Grosvenor
Square, which was supposed to be a big secret so that we were
out of the way of any anti-apartheid demos. Of course, just
about everyone knew where we were – apart from the sports-
goods manufacturers. We went to South Africa without any of
the usual gear.

The most demonstrators I ever saw at one time outside the
hotel numbered three and so we left without fuss, arrived in
Johannesburg at six in the morning, were given huge parcels
of oranges and about two million free cigarettes and set off on

a 100-mile journey to the Three Fountains hotel in the quiet town of Stilfontein. Bobby Windsor had gone down with gastro-enteritis, which was not improved by the treatment given to him on the plane by the Lions' other doctor, J.P.R.

'I'm not well,' Bobby said to him on the plane.

'Have a beer,' said J.P.R.

A few hours later Bobby went up again and said to him: 'I'm still not well.'

'Then have a gin-and-tonic,' said our fullback.

We settled into training, which surprised the South Africans. Syd Millar, the coach, had been there before and realized that if we began too hard there would be a reaction later. So it was softly softly all week and I began to get very keen on playing in the first match, against Western Transvaal at Potchefstroom. I was selected, played well and the Lions won by 59–13, which was a record. Phil Bennett got 23 points. Both marks were to be overtaken within the next few weeks as we went triumphantly towards the First Test.

We made the long journey to Windhoek for the second match against South West Africa. Getting to the hotel, we discovered they only had sandwiches. 'Steaks! steaks!' we shouted – and that's what we got for the next three days. Steaks for breakfast, steaks for lunch, steaks for dinner. We were a bit lucky to win. The heat and the altitude were problems but still, we were 10–14 down before Andy Irvine set up a try for Dick Milliken and then kicked us to a 23–16 victory.

The important match before the First Test came at Port Elizabeth the following Saturday. They were skippered by the great Hannes Marais, the captain elect of the Springboks, a good friend, a sincere man and a Christian. The trouble was that before the match, Johan Classen, the chairman of the Springboks selectors, went into the dressing room and suggested that the British didn't have a lot of stomach for the more physical side of the game. People in the dressing room claim – though I don't know if it's true – that he hinted it wouldn't be a bad idea if Eastern Province dished it out a bit. Silly man.

The battling started early on and it was clear Gareth was a

major target. Mind you, that was just one of the running battles. A South African forward referred to Mike Burton as 'Sonny' and was mysteriously found lying in a heap a few minutes later, moving Bobby Windsor to break out in a fiendish grin and say, 'A bloody cracker that was, man'.

Gareth, our skipper, asked Hannes to get his players to cut out the rough stuff. In fact he asked him twice without anything happening. 'Right,' said Gareth; 'If that's the way you want it, that's the way you can have it.' I like to think I played my part in following out the captain's instructions although what I remember most was being aggravated by a swarm of flies which kept getting into my eyes. However, I managed to manipulate the psychological boost for myself and the side. We won 28–14, and the heat was off us because the same day a French club playing against Eastern Transvaal became so involved that the referees abandoned the game twenty minutes from the end. They gained all the bad publicity, which was probably just as well because the local newspapers had some great photographs of Gordon Brown responding in good Scottish fashion to a South African who had butted him. That taught the guy that Broonie was good for something apart from the quality of his swearing during matches.

I was given a rest as the Lions ran up 97 points against the South West Districts at Mossel Bay – and they weren't trying all that hard. It was Alan Old's match. He scored 37 points, a record. But as Danie Craven said after the game, that sort of score doesn't do anybody much good and I agree with him. The serious business of honing up for the First Test came later against Western Province down in Cape Town at Newlands, a great rugby ground. The province had a back row of Coetzee, Du Plessis and McDonald, a really strong combination. We won 17–8 but were lucky. We could so easily have lost the first match of the tour because they kept drilling holes up the middle of the park.

The interesting thing was that although Phil Bennett kicked three goals he didn't have one of his better games and after Alan's points in the previous match there was clearly a problem for the selectors. My own preference would have been for the Englishman but in the end that didn't matter. Fate would decide.

It rained all the time we were in the Cape. On the Tuesday, Geechs and myself went off to watch the South African trials while the side played against the coloured team Proteas. They were really hepped up, according to the boys who played. There were early tackles, late tackles and just about every bit of kami-kaze stuff you could imagine. I don't blame them. They knew what a propaganda victory it would be for them if they won. But there was one terrible consequence.

Alan Old hadn't wanted to play in this match. He'd been on the substitute's bench when England had played the Porteas earlier. He knew what to expect. As it happened the foul was scandalous. Alan had swivelled and passed the ball seconds before this guy just ran at him, dived forward and hit him with his shoulder. Alan had relaxed with the ball away and went down in a heap. He thought his leg was broken but it wasn't. Nevertheless it was as bad a ligament injury as you'll ever see and he was helped off the field.

I didn't know about this at time. But by coincidence, as we were coming back from the trials in a taxi we saw an ambulance and who should get out but Phil Bennett.

We stopped and went across. Phil nodded inside and said 'It's Alan: he's had it.' He was almost crying himself. He felt a kind of sympathetic pain. It was a moving moment because Phil must have realized that Alan might well have claimed his Test place but he was genuinely sorry and cut up about Alan's state. It put a real damper on our celebrations that night.

So to the First Test. This is always 'make or break' time on any tour. If you win, you can go from strength to strength. If you lose there is a long haul to get back into the series. We fancied our chances for a number of reasons. We had been outscrummaging everyone – and with all the rain it was clearly going to be a day for nine-man rugby. Our pack and Gareth would see us through. The South Africans played into our hands because they played curtain-raising games on the Newlands pitch before the Test, and the field, which was a quagmire even before those matches started, was an absolute tip by the time we ran out.

We didn't fear South Africa either. They had six new caps and only two of their side had anything like the amount of experience that our lads had. And you couldn't expect Hannes Marais and Jan Ellis to carry the others.

In the end we won easily enough. Curiously we were nervous; I don't know why. But the South Africans never got within touching distance of our line and the final score of 12–3 was just about right. Phil kicked three penalties, we completely dominated the scrums and even the line-outs, and they didn't have any idea what to do. At the after-match banquet Danie Craven, presenting caps and blazers to the South Africans, made some embarrassing remarks to the players, face-to-face. He said to Chris Pope: 'This must be the first time anyone has gained a cap without touching the ball.' It was a bit out of order but we knew then that we had them totally on the run and it wasn't a question of whether we would win the series, but rather by how many matches and points. The party went on until Sunday.

The postscript to the Test was that the next match was against the Southern Universities and the management gave me the honour of captaining the Lions for the first and only time. I was slightly apprehensive because the best time to beat any touring side is in the games before or after a Test. We won, again, 26–4, in a low key effort but at least I can take a 100 per cent record as a Lions skipper with me to the grave.

One of our next stopping-off points was Rhodesia. We flew up to the Victoria Falls in two old Viscounts at some unearthly hour and a good day was had by all. We sailed on a riverboat, munched enormous steaks and took a little drink. After another coach trip we arrived in Salisbury where 10,000 people waving Union Jacks walked in a pro-British march chanting 'We are the same as you.' I roomed with Phil Bennett and he was as happy as a sand boy. They had TV in our room, while there was none in South Africa. Phil just glued himself in front of the set and went into raptures when the English football came on. I suspect that soccer's his number one sport.

Rhodesia was Fergus Slattery's place as well. He'd been there before with the Penguins and as soon as we arrived he was met by a crowd of Irish exiles and off they went for a night of merrymaking. When Slatts decides to make merry, stand back. The next we saw of him was on the following morning at the training session, smelling like a brewery. You didn't want to go near him.

One of our guides told us that the other side of the river was Zambia and terrorists had shot a nurse just the previous week. Stewart McKinney from Dungannon said: 'Just my luck to have survived ten years in Ulster and cop it over here.'

The thing about Slatts is that he is so fast that if he trains with the forwards, it's a doddle. He can walk faster than most of us can run. This particular day he must have been feeling hellish. But instead of staying with us he went away with the threequarters who were doing sprints. He matched J.J. Williams for five sprints before he collapsed. Then he got up and matched J.J. for a few more.

That spoke volumes about his pride. And it was reflected throughout the team. Even more so than in New Zealand, the Test side was picking itself but the ones left out – 'dirt-trackers' Mike Burton christened them – trained as hard as anyone. And no cliques were formed.

Against Rhodesia, Andy Irvine scored 22 points as we won 42–6. It could have been more. We met the then Prime Minister Ian Smith after the match. Rhodesia was a pleasant interlude before we went to Pretoria for the Second Test.

The South Africans were worried. Their players gathered on the Wednesday – twenty-four hours before they were officially allowed to do so under the Board rules – and when they got to their hotel, the management issued a strict edict that they were to have no contact with the outside world. They weren't even allowed to read the newspapers. Alan Old rejoined us with his leg patched up, but he was out of the tour. Earlier doubts that he would never play again had been dispelled and the South African surgeons had done a wonderful job. Mike Gibson was on the way to replace him.

It was a match in which – if we had even got half of our play on song – we would have won by over 50 points. We would have slaughtered them. After thirty minutes we were 10–0 up when by rights and on a good day we would already have been

88

double that number in front. South Africa even got it back to 10–6 but a little Phil Bennett sidestep to take him over squashed any hopes of a surprise and then Gareth set up another for 'Broonie' to dive over. With Dick Milliken scoring another it still ended up at 28–9, the worst Springbok defeat in history. Afterwards we reckoned that although we had scored five tries we had also missed another seven. And another five kicks at goal went astray. Still, it meant we couldn't lose the series. It was time for a bit of fun.

A three-day break at the Kruger National Park provided it. We flew down in a couple of very old Dakotas but there were a lot of Lions who could have flown down themselves without an aircraft. In the Scottish phrase, a lot were 'fleeing'. The latest catchphrase spreading through the side was 'There will be no sleep on this tour.' When the man from the South African breweries put a few cases of beer on the plane, the party – which had never really stopped – started again in earnest.

Mervyn Davies was determined to beat Sean Lynch's 1971 British and Irish Rugby Union Celebrating Record. I was bowling along quite nicely. We settled into the Skukuza Camp on the Game reserve, a small collection of primitive huts called rondavels, carried on drinking and that evening started one of the all-time great sessions.

It began with a game called Thumper. It's a daft pub game really. You all sit round a table and pass signs to each other. All the time you are thumping away like mad on the table. It's not exactly the kind of activity which would gain you a PhD, but it's fun. The point of the game is that if you fail to pass on the right signals, you are penalized by being made to drink a can of beer. Inevitably, the poor players get even worse the more they have to drink – and end up under the table.

It was enough to put Billy Steele away for the next twenty-four hours. Roy Bergiers cheated by pouring the drink over his head rather than down his throat. J.P.R. couldn't find his bed and slept on the floor. The game was watched by a large crowd and I tried to take a silver collection for all the fun we were giving the audience. I think I eventually got to bed myself but I'm not too sure.

The point about the camp was that all that separates you

from the jungle outside is a simple fence. Beyond there is every animal in the jungle – lions, leopards, rhino – a whole menagerie of the beasts. You could hear them roaring in the night and it was no place to be for anyone whose nerves aren't strong.

Slatts provided the best laugh after setting up Tommy David, who was genuinely nervous about the things which were going bump in the night. He waited until Tommy was in bed, then went away and got a branch from a tree. While Tommy was sleeping, he crept up to his window and started tickling him with the branch. Tommy leapt out of his bed and the first thing he saw was a Lions mascot which we had been carrying all over South Africa. Bleary-eyed, Tommy thought it was a snake – and gave it a right kicking.

Then Tom Gace hid up a tree and waited until Willie John McBride came past. Willie John, for some reason, was carrying Phil Bennett on his back and as he passed by, Tom bent down and tickled him with a twig. Willie John beat the 100 metres record with Phil shouting madly to let him down.

With Billy Steele out of the game we decided to wake him up in the traditional manner by throwing a bucket of water over him. Sandy Carmichael volunteered for the task, with some relish. But Sandy got it wrong and threw it straight over Gordon Brown which didn't amuse Broonie because he was wearing his best gear – red trousers, red shirt, red pullover. I think you get the picture of our stay at the Kruger National Park. Pity I never saw much wildlife – of the natural variety, that is.

My partner in most crimes both at Skukuza and throughout the tour was our South African liaison man, Choet Visser. Choet was some man. If anything needed fixing he would do it. Although there were no cliques, we did have our own little groups and Choet and I formed 'The Mafia'. He was the Godfather and the other members were Willie John, Slatts and Syd Miller. Choet did all the deals with the tickets and if there were any presents coming our way, he organized them. There are a lot of guys back in the United Kingdom whose houses are full of copper, skins, that sort of thing. They have Choet and the Mafia to thank for that.

All good things come to an end. The way things had gone in the camp it was probably a blessing. We needed to dry out. More importantly, the next two matches almost extracted a big penalty for our excesses. The Quaggas in Johannesburg and the Orange Free State in Bloemfontein both almost managed to bring our unbeaten record to a halt. I suppose in a long tour you need some relaxation. But the moral was that if you intended to be 100 per cent serious about rugby, there was no place for a holiday right in the middle of the tour.

I didn't play against the Quaggas, a match the Lions won 20–16. The manager Syd Millar for his own reasons stuck in all the big guys. The winning try caused an uproar because Tommy David clearly knocked on before Gordon Brown scrambled it over the line. The referee, Ian Gourlay, awarded the try and the crowd didn't like it. At the end many of them scrambled over the barriers intent on doing severe damage to the unfortunate ref, who had disallowed a couple of Quaggas tries earlier in the match. They got him to the ground and began punching him, but Broonie was hanging about and took the main culprit off to the police.

At the banquet. the chairman of the South African Referees Association, Mr Wouter de Toit, had a go at Gourlay, which was out of order. The refereeing on this tour could be criticized, especially in the interpretation of the line-out laws, but the Lions never had any complaints about bias. I should just say thanks to Ian Gourlay for his help in keeping that winning record going.

The Orange Free State was even harder. We went into the game without a recognized kicker and with ten minutes left, 65,000 Afrikaaners were in a frenzy with their side winning 9–7. It was frenzied on the field because the refereeing was inefficient and the Lions – upset by the way that the South Africans were laying across the ball in the rucks – had taken matters into their own hands. There were black eyes and split heads all over the place. Luckily we won with a try set up by a big push in a scrum against the Free State who were a man short – Stoffel Botha was off with concussion and the replacement had not yet got permission to come on. Gareth went round the blind side for J.J. to score.

The tour continued – to Griqualand, Pretoria, East London – but all the time we were waiting for the Third Test and the celebrations that would follow. We never had any doubt that we would win it because the South African deficiencies were so obvious. We would take them to pieces in the scrums, beat them in the line-outs and outrun them as well. They didn't have good enough players and their technique was suspect. In short, throughout that tour, the Lions were in a different class.

The Springboks had one card to play. They could try to sort us out physically and that's what happened in Port Elizabeth. The battle was momentous, especially after they had levelled J.P.R. There was the most massive, spectacular punch-up with McLauchlan doing his little bit again. In one of the most ugly moments, Gareth, Bobby Windsor, Willie John and Broonie were all swinging more punches than Muhammad Ali ever managed in fifteen rounds. For the first twenty minutes they put some pressure on us, but in the end we won comfortably.

The try which Gordon Brown scored summed up the difference between the two sides. The Lions were 'professional'; the Springboks weren't. Broonie simply went to the front of a line-out on the South African line; the Springboks didn't notice and threw the ball straight to him. The only man who could have stopped him diving over was their hooker, but Fran Cotton had him in a bear hug and he couldn't move. They weren't too happy when Bobby Windsor laughed out loud as Broonie lay on top of the ball after scoring.

There were two good tries from J.J. Andy Irvine kicked well and Phil Bennett dropped a couple of goals. It finished 26–9. For the first time in history the Lions had won three straight Tests and for the first time in history the South Africans had lost a series on their own soil.

As we trooped off, Sandy Carmichael came up and said: 'You won't sleep until Monday.' Back at the hotel, a big group of supporters, mainly Welsh, had gathered. We went into a private room but they kept on sending in champagne. So we asked them in and the party raged on again. We all ended up in Sandy's room, sending down occasionally for more beer.

Another group on the tour was called the Fireman's Union and they had discovered the hotel's fire hoses. As we sat in the room somebody stuck a hose round the door and turned the water on. The place was awash. Fran Cotton just sat there while the rest of us attempted to get the damn thing turned off again. He never moved except to put his hand over the top of his pint. 'I don't like watery beer,' he said.

Carmichael was as good as his word. He wouldn't let me go to bed. On the Sunday we all went out to a nearby beach and swam and drank and swam and ate and swam and drank a little bit more. What we had accomplished began to sink in. We were proud men.

I forget who said it but after we had got our heads out of the clouds someone remarked: 'C'mon, we're here to do a job of work. Let's go through the whole trip unbeaten.' No South African team had scored a try against our Saturday side for a couple of months. Neither were they to do so until the very last match of the tour. It seemed reasonable and we picked ourselves up and decided to go for the whitewash.

The hardest provincial obstacle left was Natal and that turned out to be an unfortunate game in quite a few respects. For a start there was quite a lot of arguing amongst ourselves. The backs wanted to see more of the ball but Gareth, correctly in my view, was kicking. He reasoned we only had to play the ball into the corners and then knock them about in the scrums and the line-outs. Mike Gibson was shouting 'Move it.' I was shouting back at him and we ended up at loggerheads.

Then there was the incident between Tommy Bedford and J.P.R. Bedford, the second man up to J.P.R. when he was fielding the ball, knocked him into touch. J.P.R. thought that Bedford had deliberately kicked him and replied with a few punches, and the crowd had to intervene to stop him from putting Tommy into the infirmary. Natal were only three points down with ten minutes to play and although we hadn't done as well as we could they were still physically dead. Then Phil Bennett cut loose and we scored 21 points in injury time – a record. Mind you, the ref did play an extra eleven minutes.

The nastiness spilled over after the match. They had this

guy Norton who claimed I had knocked out one of his teeth. When he turned up at the reception with his wife, she tore into me about it, face to face. He just stood by rather sheepishly. 'At least you've got more guts than he has,' I told her. The next season I played for Natal in the Currie Cup which goes to show that, whatever happens in the heat of battle, it doesn't destroy the real lasting friendships in the game.

That left just one more match for me – the Final Test against the Springboks in Johannesburg. We were staying in the best hotel I've ever been in, the Llandrost, with its own swimming pool, saunas and magnificent restaurant. Just as in New Zealand three years before, the last match was the difficult one as thoughts turned towards home. Again there were the countless letters of thanks to be written, the farewells to be said. Psychologically it was difficult to get keyed up.

Added to that was the fact that we had beaten South Africa so convincingly in the first three Tests and the mood was dangerously complacent. Victory was ours, so we thought, just as long as the bus delivered us to the right ground. In the end we managed a 13–13 draw which left us unbeaten but the Grand Slam had eluded us. We had no real cause for complaint against a Springbok side keyed up to play. Fergus Slattery seemed to have scored the winning points in the last minute when he got over the line but the referee decided – correctly – that he hadn't grounded the ball. Against that, there were doubts about one of our tries by Roger Uttley because the South Africans claimed that Chris Pope had grounded the ball before him. My disappointment was tinged with a sense of relief that Hannes had got something out of the season, because his leadership deserved it.

It was over. There was niggling criticism that the '74 side should have run the ball more and should have piled up the points against some of the weaker teams. Maybe so. But our tactics had worked and we were going home unbeaten. If the purpose of playing is winning, then we had won. Full stop. And you can't expect a forward like myself not to relish tactics based on forward power. We had done the job. It was the end of my Life with the Lions. They didn't pick me for the 1977 Tour of New Zealand. I think they made a mistake.

# IO

# Irish Jigs

Dick Milliken was one of those British Lions who never quite had enough praise heaped upon him after the South African tour. That was wrong. I remember him playing against Transvaal, cutting through inside their 25 one minute and when the move broke down, being back almost on his own line, falling in front of the entire Transvaal pack, taking a pummeling – and stopping a certain try. Dick became a good friend.

That sums up the Irish approach to rugby and an incident at Murrayfield the next season typifies all that's best in their philosophy about the game. It started in a ruck.

I burrowed in and rucked Dick Milliken out. The other Irish forwards weren't too happy about the way I had gone about it and it's true that I had stood on top of my mate at one time, accidentally of course. The most agitated was Moss Kean and if there's someone I don't fancy taking a swing at me, it's Moss. So I gripped him tight and stayed close. Out of the corner of my eye I could see Stewart McKinney coming and looking across at me. 'He's another mate,' I thought. 'He wouldn't do anything like that.' The next thing I knew he'd hit me flush on the jaw with a right, a beautiful shot. I just managed to stay on my feet.

At the dinner that night, Stewart came across and said 'McLauchlan . . . and here I was thinking you were a pal of mine.' I muttered my apologies for the tramping. 'Oh, no . . . not that,' he said, 'You were only going for the ball. But when I hit someone with my best punch I expect them to go down. Sure that's the thing to do if you are a pal.'

And that's the way it is. In all my games against the Irish I never remember a dirty one. They'll battle, in fact they battle

95

better than anyone. But their spirit is tremendous, they're great blokes and there's only one thing more serious than an Irish training session. That's an Irish drinking session.

Irish rugby is good for the game and good for the country as well. They suffer in many ways from some of the handicaps that beset Scotland. Rugby isn't the national game and they have competition not just from soccer but from hurling and Gaelic football. But no matter whether they are in the doldrums or not, they are desperately hard to beat.

I say 'good for the country' because the North-South divisions don't affect the game at all. Teams travel from the North to the South; so do supporters, referees and selectors. When the committee picks the Irish side, no one gives a twopenny damn about whether a player is an Ulsterman or not – or which church he goes to on a Sunday. The game has built bridges across the community and I've been proud, with my connections with the Wolfhounds, to have played a little part in it.

One of the worst decisions that the SRU ever made was to refuse to go and play in Dublin in 1972 after terrorists had burned down the British embassy there. It was a committee decision because I can assure you that I spoke to every member of the team and they were willing, indeed anxious to go. I would apologize to all my friends for that.

The troubles can have their funny side. I was invited to Belfast to play in a game commemorating the opening of Instonians' new clubhouse. Andy Ripley was also in the select side and, as usual, Andy was late. He left a message that he would catch the next plane from Heathrow and we started the match without him. After a few minutes play, there was this terrific noise and as the packs looked up we saw a helicopter hovering over the field. The other prop Paddy Agenew shouted to me 'Pray to God McLauchlan that it's one of ours.' In fact it was Andy arriving in some style, courtesy of the British army.

I'd go back any time, just send the invitation. I'd want to be part of a game which stands above and outside the politics of Ireland and shows how people can get on together. They are my sort of people.

I had good reason to afford the Irish every respect. In the first match I played against them at Murrayfield, Scotland lost 17–5. Two years later in the same fixture, I broke my leg. I've only been on the winning side at Landsdowne Road once, in 1976.

They play with this Gallic fervour and they have the awful ability to reduce any match to a state of complete and total disorder in which all your pre-match tactics fly straight out of the window. It's very cunning. For example, whereas other sides might put one man over the ball in the ruck and get penalized for the infringement, the Irish think nothing of putting all eight men over the top. That leaves the referee thinking that the whole pack is legitimately looking for the ball and he'll only award a scrum.

For long enough they never had a good line-out jumper so they worked a simple thing with their own throws. They would let the other side take the ball and then all walk through and give stick to the opposition scrum-half. Then in 1973 they discovered Kevin Mays, who could jump and catch. 'Sure Ian,' said one of his teammates, 'Kevin is getting us all into trouble. He's catching the ball but by that time we're all through on the scrum-half and it's offside again.'

I don't mean to say that the Irish are slap-happy or that they are a bunch of softies. With Willie John McBride, Moss Kean, Sean Lynch and Stew McKinney around they are anything but that. They'll give as good as they get. And Ray McLoughlin had a tremendous influence on their tactics, making sure that they won the scrums, won the ball and made good, sound use of it. They are very intense about the game and if it is going to be a physical battle, then they'll be steaming in, no danger. In the best rugby sense, they are fighters to a man.

There's a lovely atmosphere in Dublin on match days. We usually stayed in the same hotel as the Irish (the Shelbourne), though on different floors. Once, the telephone in my room went on the Friday morning. It was McLoughlin. 'Sure,' he said, 'it's nice to talk to you; I gather you've got a sore leg.' I had nothing of the sort.

On the Saturday morning the phone went again and it was

the same man. 'Now I've been checking this out on the grapevine and I'm told that your leg is even worse; in fact you're limping. I'll see you this afternoon and I'll be waiting for you,' he said. I even thought I had a bad leg myself after that piece of gentle blarney.

Willie John was something again: this huge, gentle man, usually smoking his pipe. Ian McGeechan has reason to remember him more than most. On the Lions tour of South Africa, we learned about the famous Willie John tactics talks which invariably ended with him going round the dressing room punching all his teammates and urging them into action. The Irish were used to it and would cover up their chest and arms when they saw McBride approach. Ian didn't know about it and in his first match Willie John's playful punch ended up with Geechs being sent sprawling over the dressing room chair. 'That was the hardest anyone hit me on the whole tour,' he would say later.

Tom Grace was a match for him. When Willie John broke the Irish record for the greatest number of caps, it was decided to make a presentation and, as we were in town, Scotland were invited as well. They had collected for a beautiful Cork crystal plate, inscribed and embellished, a piece of art which must have cost a fortune. After it had been presented, the plate was passed round as Willie puffed contentedly on his pipe. Next thing, there is a terrible noise of breaking glass. 'Oh, Willie John, I've just dropped it,' Tom says. There was a deafening silence. 'I'm sorry,' adds Grace: 'I'll make it up to you.' Willie John said not to bother and tried to look nonchalant but was inwardly boiling. Grace kept it up for a long time before admitting he had hidden the glass plate and dropped one of the hotel dishes on the floor. That's the Irish for you.

Fergus Slattery was just as daft – the untidiest man in the world. Slatts would come into a room and there would be chaos five minutes later. I shared with him in New Zealand and it was like living with a walking rubbish dump. Once he went off to a reception wearing Chris Rea's trousers and Chris must be four inches shorter. A lovely man.

I'm not going into individual matches simply because that isn't what Irish rugby is all about. It's about spirit and sportsmanship. Rather than remember the ones we won and the ones we lost, I'd like to take to my deathbed the most treasured moment of all. It happened in 1973 and the game ended in a narrow Scottish win, 19–14.

Dougie Morgan took a drop at goal and the referee was unsighted and uncertain whether to award the points or not. He was helped out of that dilemma by Tom Kiernan, that marvellous fullback. Tom raised his hand acknowledging that the score was correct and those points were the turning-point of the match.

When you play with people like that, the winning and the losing doesn't matter quite so much. It's simply been a privilege to be on the same field. The Irish don't have or need luck. They've something much better. It's called style.

# The Auld Alliance

All that's good in rugby can be seen in France. All that's bad in rugby can be seen in France as well. Some of the stuff they get up to gives the game exactly the image that it can do without. So this is a short chapter.

In 1971 I went to Paris for the first time with Scotland. On the Thursday night I went to the Folies Bergères and enjoyed it – the best part of the trip. On the Saturday night I ended up at Harry's Bar and that wasn't a bad thrash either. In between wasn't so good.

We were doing well when the French hoisted a long kick towards Sid Smith, our full back. Sid fielded it and kicked into touch. Then relaxed. He was hit – so late it was unbelievable – by Jean Pierre Bastiat and had to go off. It was exactly the type of incident that ruins the game; so open and unnecessary. In the reshuffle, Brian Simmers came on at fly-half and Jock Turner went back. That upset our plan to stop Pierre Villepreux which had been working up to that point, and we ended up losers, 13–8.

That wasn't the only time down the years that we had trouble with the French. 1975 was a real classic. In the first line out there was a good old contretemps involving about a dozen of us. Immediately the referee called across Sandy Carmichael and Bofelli and warned them: the next bit of trouble and they would be off. The problem was that just about the only two who hadn't been wading in was that pair.

What developed was a very private battle between myself and Monsieur Gerard Cholley. It started when he tried to gouge one of my eyes out. I felt this fingernail biting across the top of my cheek. I asked Gordon Brown what the French word for 'eyes' was because I wanted to have a few words with Monsieur Cholley. '*Oeufs*,' replied Broonie, the silly so-and-so. I ended up telling Cholley that I wasn't prepared to have my eggs knocked out and even that lost a bit in the translation. So he did it again and I gave him the boot. In fact I gave him the boot twice.

Still, he didn't get the message. He dragged his hand across my cheek again and I thought that if I was going to finish the match with my eyesight intact, I would have to finish this Frenchman first. So I gave him the boot again. At last he got the message that I was determined that if one of us was going to finish the match, that one was going to be McLauchlan.

'We won the battle, but lost the match,' was how Bill Dickinson described it afterwards and with Duncan Madsen fighting with their hooker I got dragged into most of the action. At one stage the French used me as a doormat and the whole pack went over the top of me in a very cynical working over. They ripped the shorts and socks off me as they went. I couldn't sit down for a fortnight after that – and sad to say, some of my teammates were not amazingly quick at coming to my assistance.

It's like this. I've said it before and I'll say it again, I abhor dirty play. I'm very clear where the dividing line is between a legitimate battle and an outrageous foul. But when you are representing your country you cannot just lie down and take it. If that's the way the rules are going to be for the afternoon, then you've got to go to war. You are not just representing yourself after all; you are playing for a nation and a way of life. You hope the referee will sort it out and sort it out quickly. In the meantime, you play the rules as they are being played against you.

The French will always play to those limits. I think that they deliberately do it just to see how you respond to a bit of nonsense. And they are past-masters at the professional foul. They know all about obstruction and they will always try to play inside the ten-yard line at free kicks. Nothing illustrates that better than an incident against Ireland when Tony Ward was given a kick in front of the French posts. As he retreated with the ball the French just walked up the field after him and when he took the kick, it was charged down. For this to happen to a man of his class is impossible – that is if the French had stayed back ten yards.

In 1977, I had to sit on the bench and watch Scotland be first intimidated and then humiliated by the French, who were again at the dirty stuff. With the same Monsieur Cholley in the middle of it all. After the game, which France not surprisingly won 23–3, their president Albert Ferasse singled him out for a rebuke and said that if he did it again he would find himself out of the side. The Frenchman punched Donald MacDonald, he punched Jim Renwick and felled Ron Wilson with what was supposed to be a fend-off. The referee Meirion Joseph allowed him to stay on the field.

So upset was the SRU president Hector Munro that he said at the banquet: 'The game is bigger than the players and those who will not conform must be weeded out. I leave this serious thought with you not to sleep upon but to act upon.'

This is a short chapter because what Hector – now Minister of Sport – said was absolutely correct. The French are admired for their running skills and, Wales apart, have more natural talent than any other country. Off the field I like them. When I pick my World XV you will see that the number of French players in the reckoning is considerable. But I don't want to go and fight battles, whether the war is won or lost. I want to play a hard – very hard – brand of rugby by the laws of the game, and not by the rules of the corner-boy. Let's just leave it at that.

# 12

# The Good Times

I'm not envious in any way of a sportsman like Kevin Keegan who can make a million out of playing football. No rugby player I have ever met wanted to play for pay. Keegan lives in a goldfish bowl; he is continually under pressure to play well and an injury at any time could end not just his career but his earning power as well. The rugby player is free from those kind of worries and prefers to be. I don't see full-time professional rugby ever coming and that's not just because the unions would fight tooth and nail to prevent it. I don't think the players would want it either. Any guy deciding to take up rugby knows what he can and cannot expect out of the game and if money matters to him, then he can take up some other sport.

That said, the player wants to be treated in a professional manner and often isn't. Let's take some examples of how the SRU fail to give the players the respect they deserve. For a start, too often the travelling arrangements for Scottish teams are made with more regard to the officials than the needs of the men who will be going out and battling for their country.

Whenever Scotland play at Twickenham we stay at the Charing Cross Hotel right in the middle of London. It's a few yards away from the Strand and close enough to Soho, if you're that way inclined. Just how can the side prepare themselves in that kind of atmosphere?

It's the same in Wales. The traditional hotels for us to stay in are the Park or the Angel – which is only 110 yards from the National Stadium. My own form of preparation before any big match is to get up late and look for a bit of peace and quiet so that I can start concentrating. But everywhere you turn –

inside the hotel as well as outside – the place is packed with fans wanting your autographs, and keen to discuss the forth-coming match with you. When last season the SRU decided to move out of Cardiff, they got it partly right and chose a hotel one-and-a-half hours' drive from the game in Chepstow. But the real bind was to have to go back there on the Saturday night. We should have stayed in Cardiff.

The odd thing about the SRU is that they are generous to a fault in some matters – and niggardly in others. Before an international at Murrayfield we always stay in a small family hotel in Edinburgh where the food is substantial, maybe too substantial. I know I've eaten too much at times. No expense is spared there. And if you want to go off on a Friday afternoon to play golf or billiards, then the taxis and mini-buses are laid on.

And the after-match hospitality is unrivalled anywhere in the world. Eileen knows I am a big eater but even she would be surprised at the damage I've done to the scotch broth, the haggis, the roast beef and all the trimmings after many a Murrayfield game.

But in other ways they can be quite unbelievably stingy. Up until two years ago for example, you got one jersey and then had to pay for the rest at £10 to £12 a time. It's traditional to swop them and I have always done so. There's a complete set of world jerseys up in the attic and I regard them as rewards beyond price for all my efforts over the seasons. The SRU obviously think that thousands would give their right arms just to get one of the jerseys and that we should see it the same way – and then write out the cheque. I happen to think we deserve them and the SRU have come round to see it that way. But we still have to supply our own shorts and stockings every time we play for Scotland. And the record books may show that I have forty-three Scottish caps, but don't take that too literally. I have only one. That's SRU – and general rugby – policy as well. You get the cap after your first appearance for Scotland – and that's it.

And on tour, too, the SRU can be mean. When we toured Japan in 1977, the side was absolutely broke. Literally broke. The funds had run so low that the basic necessities like laundry just couldn't be done. At the time it seemed like a minor inconvenience but when you look back on the amount of money that the Japanese were taking through the gates, it was criminal.

For years I suppose I broke one of the basic rules of amateurism, as defined by the SRU, in the matter of not paying for my gear. It was all supplied by Adidas and for free. The SRU must have known – they would have been idiotic if they hadn't – but they chose to turn a blind eye to the matter.

It all started in a rather hilarious way in Paris. One year when we were there, Rodger Arneill said that he had permission to approach Adidas, who had agreed in turn to kit us out. Whether he had permission or not I wouldn't know, but he said he had. So the negotiations started in a mixture of pidgin French and pidgin English for the upshot was that we thought Adidas would kit us out for 50p each, which seemed a bargain. Later the same day we trooped into Rodger's room where all the gear was laid out – boots, tracksuits, wetsuits, the complete set. And standing there was a Frenchman with a huge wad of notes. He thought the deal was that we would play in the gear as long as Adidas would pay us 50 francs each. The boys were horrified. 'We can't take money,' they shouted. 'The gear's great, we'll wear it for nothing.'

Over the years, I established quite a connection with them. But all the business had to be done on the quiet and my house was sometimes full of pairs of boots sent to me by Adidas.

The SRU really should get this organized on an official basis for one good reason. Any sports goods manufacturer doing a little bit of sponsorship on the side is always interested in having his gear worn by the star players, especially the backs who are seen most often on TV. Quite often, it has ended up with some players getting well looked after – and the others getting nothing. If the SRU were involved officially it would ensure that the whole thing was done on a fairer footing. Everyone would get the same amount of equipment and that would help to build team spirit.

But those points apart, I'm happy to have played for the rewards I have received, rewards which can't be measured in terms of money. Any sportsman who at the end of his career can say that he has been to South Africa and New Zealand, Canada, the USA, Japan and the Far East can look back on a host of memories. Mind you, I'm not sure that the best tour of the lot wasn't a great deal nearer home – in Ireland.

It was 1974. We had arrived back from South Africa, had a summer's rest and were invited to Dublin to celebrate the Irish Rugby Union's centenary in a match at Landsdowne Road between Ireland and Scotland against England and Wales. Most of the Lions were there and the match was good fun, ending in a draw. What followed was a monumental night, the kind of thrash I don't suppose you could have anywhere else in the world.

For most of the boys that was OK. The trouble was that I had been made captain of the Irish Wolfhounds who were to continue the centenary celebrations by touring the country – starting against Munster in Waterford the very next day. Now if there's one place you don't want to be playing with a hangover it's in Munster. They don't hang back. They give the game about 100 per cent commitment and when you are hit you stay hit. By the time they had rounded us up in the morning and got the bus moving it was obvious we were late. In fact we arrived at the ground with about ten minutes to spare. J.J., Tony Nearey, Bobby Windsor and I were all playing with most of the rest of the Wolfhounds side made up of Frenchmen. Gareth and Phil Bennett were also supposed to be in the team but although they travelled down there, they decided against playing. Sensible chaps.

We got beaten. But I remember the match for one of those instances which prove what a great game rugby can be. The night before, Terry Moore, the Irish number eight, had bought me a pint of Guinness. This should have qualified for that company's book of records because Terry was well known for his ability to hang on to coin. In fact, when I told some of his teammates that Terry had bought me a drink, they claimed it must have been a dream. Anyway at Waterford, Terry and I are buried at the bottom of a maul and as all hell breaks loose round about me, he whispers: 'McLauchlan, you owe me a pint.'

Later on that tour there was a match against Connaught on

what was literally a cowfield in a place called Ballina. That was memorable because of the speech the local mayor gave after the match: 'We are honoured that such famous rugby people as Mickey Mouse have come to play in our town.' As Barry McGann said in reply: 'You should see Donald Duck.' All in all, a super tour, full of friendships, full of Irish hospitality and I'll never forget the time I ordered trout and steak for dinner – and they were served on the same plate.

A year later I was invited back to South Africa to coach the Durban club Northlands and the local Boys High School. That was an honour and the bonus was that Eileen and the boys went with me to a hotel on the beach just outside the city. J.J. and J.P.R. were on the same trip and Fran Cotton was coaching the University side. It seemed pointless not to play as well as coach and I ended up in the Currie Cup, playing for Natal against Eastern Transvaal. Also in a friendly against Transvaal – which I must mention because I scored a try. The kids still talk about it, just another reason to be glad of what rugby has done for me.

In 1975, Scotland were invited to tour New Zealand. It was a trip that really should have taken place before but the SRU had turned it down and England went instead. That was quite wrong because you can't afford to turn down any chance of gaining international experience and there's no place better to learn than in New Zealand. England had taken our place in 1972 but at least we eventually went back.

I had spoken to David Duckham about that England tour. 'You'll never believe how "small time" it is compared to the Lions trip,' he said.

It was – but it was also the happiest Scottish tour of all time. George Burrell and Bill Dickinson, the management, ensured it was trouble-free. The lads were tremendous. When the total damage bill was totted up at the end it came to the princely sum of 35p – and that was after one of the guys knocked over a bedside table by accident and broke the light bulb.

Its spirit was summed up by David Bell, who should earn himself a permanent place in rugby records as the man who travelled furthest to play one match. Unfortunately David got injured against Otago but was kept on the tour as a 'Sibbalds Member.' Sibbalds was the name of the SRU travel agents.

The problem was what to do to keep David happy – and it was decided to make him an extra man in the management team. As he said at the end: 'Since becoming management, the amount of gin-and-tonic which I've been forced to drink on this trip has set my career back years.' That was the sort of time it was – the playing was serious, the patter was great.

I had the mickey taken out of me for weeks. As a New Zealand tour veteran I was supposed to know it all and had been telling the team for days that a highlight of the tour would come in Napier before the Hawkes Bay match. In 1971, the town turned out in procession before the game. There must have been about forty floats depicting various ways that we would get slaughtered, and the parade stretched for a couple of miles or more. 'Wait until you see it,' I kept saying. On the great day we looked out of our hotel – and there it was, one single float showing the Loch Ness monster. I didn't live that one down even to the end.

The very good spirit, in fact, created problems. No one wants to travel round the world and hardly play a match and this Scottish group was no exception. Added to that, guys who really didn't have much chance of making the Test team were making huge contributions both on and off the pitch. Really we should have settled on the Test side early on and let it play together. But for understandable reasons we didn't do so and our results suffered because of it.

We won the opener against Nelson Bays, then lost to Otago and Canterbury in matches we should have won. Billy Steele was tackled diabolically in the first of these two games, but the referee chose not to see it and in the second we were leading, missed a few chances and fell away. But the great thing about Canterbury was that the troubles in 1971 were all forgotten and the New Zealanders there went out of their way to make sure we had a good time. We won well against Wellington – one of the best games in which I have ever played. The sun

Against Australia, 1975. A good push and the cork will pop

Not too many Frenchmen in sight as I reach for this ball at Murrayfield

Bobby Windsor addresses the 1974 Lions

Sandy and myself give Bill Dickinson a helping hand

A win over Wales – and Gerald is the first to congratulate me as
Gordon Strachan looks on

The Calcutta Cup is back in its proper hands, 1976

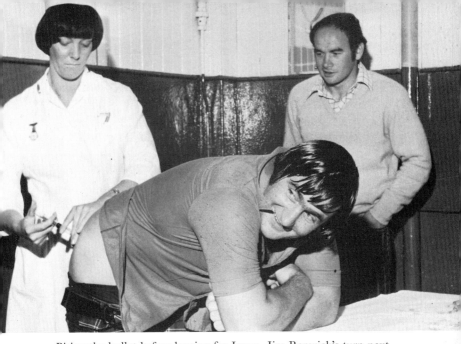

Biting the bullet before leaving for Japan. Jim Renwick's turn next

The gunslinger

I must have hit a straight one for a change. Chris Rea couldn't believe it

Pity Jock Stein wasn't around

The Mouse in drag. The Ugly Sister in the school panto. Pity Sandy wasn't there to play the other half

Tackling Fergus Slattery – against Ireland in 1978

Grounded against the Irish, 1978

shone, we ran the ball, they ran it and there were tries and penalties at both ends. Dougie Morgan was anointed, kicking six out of six and that saw us through.

At Hawkes Bay, where we won as well, I remember a single incident which had important long-term significance for Scotland. One of the opposition props broke forward and advanced on Colin Fisher. We expected Colin to get minced, but he stood his ground, made a truly great tackle and although he was hurt, the other New Zealand guy was in as big a mess. It was a sign that a new hooker had arrived, determined to play for his country. He had won his spurs.

A win against Bay of Plenty carried us into the Test Match that should never have been played. The circumstances, however, were all against the New Zealand Rugby Union. In Auckland, there had been a tropical storm overnight and Eden Park was under four inches of water. Only a small patch in the middle of the field stood above the waves. If it had been any ordinary match no one would have even considered playing but the trouble was that New Zealanders had been arriving from all over the country and we had to go home straight afterwards. So it was agreed to play the Water Polo Test.

Scotland lost 24–0, four tries to nil and on paper that doesn't look too hot. All it really meant was that the All Blacks were better at underwater rugby than we were. Sandy Carmichael was panicking because he couldn't swim and there was one incident that could have been extremely serious when Colin Fisher got trapped at the bottom of a ruck with about twelve lads on top of him. His whole face was under the water and he thought he would drown. I could believe it.

Bruce Hay, in his first cap, broke an arm. If it had been a dry day I honestly think that we would have given the All Blacks one hell of a run for their money and I wouldn't have ruled out beating them. But it was still a happy party who flew back home. You don't always judge the success or otherwise of tours by results. Friendship and fun matter just as much – and we'd had plenty of those two commodities.

There were even happier times to come. In 1977 Scotland

were invited to tour the Far East and Japan – and that was just as good. The previous year, Wales had been out there and given the Japanese a right pasting. So we were asked to take out a 'half-and-half' squad, a smattering of top guys combined with some up-and-coming players. That wasn't too difficult to do because the Lions were touring in New Zealand at the same time and we were without Andy Irvine, Ian McGeechan, Gordon Brown and Bruce Hay. Mike Biggar was captain and Nairn McEwan, after his success with Highland, was made player coach.

It was a well-prepared Scotland squad as well. We had some good pre-tour sessions and every player was asked to meet training and fitness schedules. It might have been only Japan, who couldn't be rated as in the top League, but there was no Mickey Mouse approach by us.

I shared a room with a great character, Gerry McGuinness of West of Scotland. When we arrived on the first stop, Bangkok, the temperature was over 100° F and the humidity was incredible. To make matters worse, the air-conditioning wasn't working in the hotel. 'Christ, it's hot,' I said. 'That's OK,' replied Gerry – and went and opened the window, which made it twice as bad. 'Where I come from, when it's too hot we always open the window,' he said.

Poor Gerry. Another time we were taken to this very swish restaurant for dinner and the first course was prawns served on a lotus leaf – a very prickly leaf indeed. Gerry must have been hungry. He polished off the prawns and then the lotus leaf as well. He couldn't speak. His mouth was on fire. They led him away as quietly as possible.

We played a Thai XV in Bangkok and Mighty Mouse was bigger than anyone on the opposing side, the only time that's ever happened before or since. We won easily. And all I'll say about the rest of that visit is that if I ever wished to commit suicide, then I would just go to Bangkok and let it all happen for a couple of weeks. Then I'd be dead.

Hong Kong was just as hot – and the referee seemed to have been following the rules as they were in 1939. And then it was on to Japan where we played three matches and won the lot, including the Test in Tokyo's Olympic Stadium, the largest ground on which I have ever played rugby. There was a 30,000 crowd and it looked lost. The tour was a forcing ground for several players and in that Test Match Roy Laidlaw and John Rutherford showed the form that was to take them into the Scottish side for the Five Nations Championships in the next few years.

We won. There was never any doubt that we were taking it seriously. A few moments from the end Bill Gammell, who had already scored three tries, was galloping in for the fourth. I was up in support and shouted for the pass. It duly came and I scored a try which could well have been his. I was grateful for it, but Alistair Cranston ran up the field shouting 'McLauchlan, if you had dropped that ball, I would have killed you.' Or words to that effect.


I had always wanted to show Eileen New Zealand. For six years she had heard me going on week after week about how great a place it had been in 1971. The chance came when I was invited out, along with Jim Renwick and Andy Irvine, to be a guest of Zingari Richmond, a Dunedin club celebrating its centenary. And we were asked to bring along the good ladies. That made it a fun trip – and the rugby was good value too. I was a member of a World XV, loosely named, because it consisted of five Fijians, three Scots and seven New Zealanders. We played three matches and in the first, at Carisbrook, I scored a try on the same ground in that memorable First Test with the Lions.

The big match was against the New Zealand Barbarians at Eden Park and it was that game which finally proved to me what I had known for a long time – the great love of the game in that country. The Ba Ba's were virtually a New Zealand side and against us were some old adversaries . . . men like Frank Oliver, Brad Johnson and Andy Dalton. They realized that if they took us on in the scrums for real, life for McLauchlan and a few others would be tough, to say the least. So we had a little meeting before the match and it was decided that each team would win its own scrummage ball and that there wouldn't be any messing about. The result was as good a game as I have every played in, full of handling rugby. The pity was that in the last match – against Wellington – I got hurt in a late tackle. But that was an exception. It was all highly enjoyable. Not just for me – but for the long-suffering Eileen and three wide-eyed boys.

# 13

# Sandy and Co.

Rugby is about people and friendships. It's also about a whole lot of laughs. Tensed up and unsmiling in the Murrayfield dressing room, the Scottish team looked fearsome. On the pitch, faced by the Welsh red jerseys, there weren't many moments when we all fell about belly-laughing. But at other times, fun was the name of the game.

The Famous Five of the Scottish Mean Machine were, in my opinion, the best scrummaging unit of modern times. I was proud to be a part of it. They were all characters.

The first time that the front row came together was years back – in West of Scotland's Second XV. It's not generally known – and I don't exactly go about shouting the fact from the rooftops – that I played a season for West, Jordanhill's deadliest rivals. Just put it down to youthful aberration. It was there I met up with Sandy and Quintin Dunlop, the hooker who should have got more Scottish caps than he did.

Sandy was – and is – a lovely man. My last cap against New Zealand in 1979 carried me past him as the most capped Scottish player in history, but that includes British Lions Tests. If you limit the statistic to games played in a dark blue jersey Sandy still leads and, rightly, he cherishes that honour.

I've never met a more even-tempered fellow in rugby. In many ways, Sandy is everything I am not and probably that's why we made such a good partnership. If I am ready most times to make the quick quip, Sandy is on the dour side. He doesn't say much but when he does, it takes most people by surprise. He has an alarming habit of stating the obvious with great sincerity. We used to break up in fits.

In South Africa, it was Syd Millar's habit to invite players to take part in the team talks. Syd would outline what he expected us to do, then ask the team if they had anything to add, or whether they had picked up any local knowledge which might help. We were playing against Border in a stadium which has two massive stands but which is open at both ends. Syd asked for comments – and Sandy, who had been thinking hard for a long time, indicated that he wanted to speak. We all held our breath.

'I was talking to a guy last night,' Sandy said, 'and he told me that the wind would blow either up or down the field.' Collapse of many stout parties, but you could see what he meant. Well, roughly.

I used to dig him up something rotten. 'Sandy,' I would ask: 'what school did you go to?' He always fell for it.

'Loretto.'

'Did your parents ever think of suing it under the Trades Descriptions Act?'

But the point about Sandy was that he was just about the best-natured guy in the side. In 1977, I was recalled to the team after being dropped and the phone rang at home. It was Sandy. 'I wondered if you would like me to come and pick you up and take you over to the Braidhills Hotel,' he said. I replied that this was indeed an honour. I thought he would be motoring across with his pals from West of Scotland. 'I am, actually,' he replied: 'but we thought we would call in on our way. It's so long since you were in the Scottish team, we thought you might have forgotten your way.'

Sandy has always been a lovely man to call a friend, except when you are flying. Once, on a trip from Nelson Bays to Wellington, the pilot decided to bank in order to give us all a good view of a school of whales in the sea below us. Sandy, nervous as a kitten, immediately thought that we were going to crash as the plane slowed to one side. It was the only time I ever saw him stand up in an aircraft. He grabbed the hostess in panic, those huge mitts of his leaving the poor girl with bruises on her arm for months afterwards. The public thought Sandy and I were inseparable. That's the way I would like it to be when we're both old gnarled men, propping up the bar and boring the youngsters with tales of what it was like in the good old days.

In the second row there were two completely different characters – Al McHarg and Gordon Brown. Al was frank in the extreme and there are a good few who have wilted before one of his tongue lashings. We were playing in this district match between Glasgow and the Anglo Scots and he had flown up from London to take part. The game was tight and the turning point came when Hugh McHardy broke, passed to Richie Dixon and Richie went over for a try. The pass was about a mile forward but the referee didn't see it. At the end, Al sought out the luckless ref who thought he was about to be congratulated by this famous Scottish forward. Not so. 'I have travelled 400 miles to get here and play in this match and have to travel another 400 miles to get home,' Al thundered. 'And the game has been totally spoiled by yourself. You are incompetent. In fact you are a bloody cheat.' Exit a flabbergasted referee. But it showed how seriously Al took his rugby and I love the man for that. For years he was the best line-out man in Great Britain but the selectors discarded him far too early. His only mistake was to become, like myself, officially regarded as a veteran when he was anything but.

Gordon Brown was entirely different. His boyish good looks persuaded a lot of opponents that he wouldn't hurt a fly. That was their first mistake. Broonie was a real hard case and wouldn't stand any messing about. From anyone. Me included.

One season, Jordanhill were toiling and we rather needed the points when our match against West – with Sandy and Broonie – came round. A few nights before I had been joking with Sandy's wife that she shouldn't expect her man to come home in one piece on the Saturday night. It was a joke because there's no way that I would ever have tangled with Sandy.

As it happened, as we peeled away from an early line and made off across the pitch, I felt this hand grabbing at the back of my shirt. I thought it was my old sparring partner Bob Haldane, so I turned round without looking and hit him a cracker of a right, flush on the jaw. It was one of my better shots. To my horror, I realized that I had hit Sandy. When I got over the shock I started to see the funny side of it and burst out laughing. I could hardly run with my sides splitting. Unfortunately Broonie had seen the whole thing and didn't think it was a joking matter. A few minutes later it was my misfortune to have to go down on a loose ball and the West pack, led by Broonie, went over the top of me like a herd of rhinos. When I got up, my jersey was in tatters and my back felt like a well-ploughed field. I looked up and there was the same Mr Brown grunting and snorting and shouting: 'That showed the little fart.' I'm not saying he stood on me but half my jersey seemed to be hanging to his studs. Half my skin as well.

In all the years, I only ever saw Broonie intimidated once and that was by Willie John McBride. It was their turn in New Zealand to share a bedroom. 'Do you snore?' Willie John asked.

'Certainly not,' said Broonie, who happens to be just about the worst snorer in the world.

'I hate men who snore,' added Willie John. 'If you snore I will punch you.' The next day Broonie got up looking like a washed out rag. 'I was so afraid of snoring that I never slept a wink all night,' he said. That from a man who could never be put down on the pitch.

The Mean Machine has three hookers: Quintin, Duncan Madsen and Colin Fisher. I would be hard pushed to say who was the best. They all did everything that was required of them – and more. Duncan could be a scream. We were on tour with Scotland in New Zealand and Duncan, in for one match, was working himself into a terrible lather in the dressing room. That was his style. He would wrap a cocoon around himself and work himself up into a state, breathing fire and brimstone, generally getting into a mood to do some damage. This time, he took a terrible kick at the lavatory door which promptly fell off its hinges. The next game he was dropped and wasn't happy about it.

'Why am I dropped?' he demanded of coach Bill Dickinson.

'Well, you have to do a bit more than kick down cludgie doors to prove that you should play for Scotland,' he replied.

Rodger Arneill was another whom men of sound mind approached with some caution. He was so tall, handsome and debonair: off the field a Dr Jekyll, a perfect gentleman who could charm birds out of the trees. But the thought of a rugby match brought out the Mr Hyde in his character. I was sharing with him before one game and about three o'clock in the morning I woke up to see him running on the spot in the bedroom. I watched fascinated. Then suddenly he took off and threw himself at one of the legs of the bed, tackling it. It was a great tackle as well. He saw me watching this and muttered 'Sorry mate.' He climbed back into his bed and was fast asleep inside ten seconds. I lay awake for an hour wondering what sort of man this was. Was I safe? I asked myself.

Nairn McEwan and Mike Biggar were other members of that memorable pack. Mike I had a lot of time for. It's not everyone as posh as him who can become one of the lads and a good captain. 'Let's push at this thing and not poke at it,' he would encourage us. 'Let's nudge, chaps!' he would add. His balding head made him a fair target in the rucks and he's been on the wrong end of a lot of dubious play. But he always bounced up.

As for Nairn, he was the ultra suave Highland gentleman. There's been no one like him since he retired. Nairn was the surest tackler for many a day, a great mauler. In fact he had everything, though some people thought he was a couple of inches too short. I don't see what difference that makes. It was a scandal he didn't go on the Lions tour to South Africa in 1974. When they hand out the MBE's Nairn should be near the top of the list, considering all the sacrifices he made over the years, especially as coach to the Scotland team later on.

I had pals in the backs too. I'm not snobbish! Dougie Morgan, the scrum-half, was one of my sort of people. He wouldn't put up with any messing about; he was very definitely the sort of guy you didn't want to tangle with. Once I went through the line-out and happened to kick him on the hand. Straight away he turned round and kicked me on the knee. I apologised and said that it had been an accident. 'You kicking me on the hand was about as much of an accident as me kicking you on the knee,' he came back. He gave his all – and wasn't shy in offering advice all round. A great competitor.

So too was James Menzies Renwick, one of the funniest guys. Jim lives in Gala and plays for Hawick, which means that he's on the receiving end of stick every day in the Borders. He was once asked by a supporter why he didn't play for Gala. 'I'd rather be a lamppost in Hawick than captain of Gala,' he responded. That sums up all the rivalry which makes Borders rugby different from anything else in the world.

The great debate in Scottish rugby over the years has been whether Andy Irvine or Bruce Hay should be the fullback. I always thought we should have played both of them there and revolutionized our tactics to make that possible.

Bruce can be devastatingly funny but even he was at a loss for a word when he was presented to the Duke of Edinburgh at Twickenham before the 1979 match. Brucie has taken a few knocks and even he wouldn't say that his nose is the most beautiful feature about him. 'Have you run into a lamppost lately?' the Duke enquired. Brucie said nothing then, but that member of the Royal Family famed for his blunt speaking might have relished the retort Bruce made when he moved safely out of earshot.

Andy's an enigmatic character. He's either the hero or the villain, even in the space of a single match. Sometimes I think that he has escaped the kind of criticism that would have been meted out to others after a bad match. But you have to balance that with his ability to turn a match singlehanded. The French game in 1980 proved that. You couldn't consider him to be anything other than a truly great player after that performance.

It would have been possible to play a double fullback game. Indeed we almost did so during my last season, but decided against it at that last minute. Bruce would be my man nearer the line because he is the more powerful in the tackle and, apart from J.P.R., I can't think of a surer man standing under the high kick with the forwards coming down on top of him. But Andy has the flair with the loose ball and turning defence into attack. With both players unhappy on the wing we should have accommodated them both in the fullback roll as conditions demanded. If they had to fight the issue out, I think Bruce would have been the loser.

But do you want to know the greatest character of all in Scottish rugby? She would have made a great player.

Jordanhill were down at Gala one day before the Leagues started and we were anxious to gain recognition. We were playing our hearts out and when John Henderson kicked a lovely up-and-under out to the standside wing, I went after it like a startled rabbit. The winger was standing waiting.

'Good' I thought: 'I will put this one away.' And whacked him with a beauty of a tackle. He fell under the barrier and I was still on top of him. The only trouble was that as we fell I realized he hadn't fielded the ball at all. I thought I had better do something because they tend not to like that sort of thing happening to their own players even accidentally at Gala. I got up and extended my hand to help the winger to his feet. Suddenly this lady had stormed up to the incident and whacked me across the back with her umbrella.

It was Arthur Brown's Mum.

# 14

# Match of the Century

Murrayfield is jam-packed. Ten times the number of tickets could have been sold. In Edinburgh's North British hotel, Welsh, South African and New Zealand accents mingle with the soft Scottish burr. In one corner voluble Frenchmen are arguing and gesticulating with their hands. They are bidding £1000 for a pair of tickets for the centre stand.

Special trains are arriving by the minute from Cardiff, London and Glasgow. Old friends are meeting each other, preparing for the day with the odd gin-and-tonic – or three. Outside in Princess Street, special editions of the newspapers are on sale to commemorate the Match of the Century.

In hotels on the outskirts of the Scottish capital, thirty of the world's best rugby players are lingering over breakfast, reading the same papers. At some length Norman Mair of the *Scotsman* is propounding the theory that the Rest of the World will beat Great Britain and Ireland. The Fleet Street scribes are adamant that it will be a home win.

Outside the day is crisp and clear. The early morning frost has gone and the sun is beginning to peek out from behind Arthur's Seat. I ring Eileen – at home on the other side of the city – and tell her to arrive early at Murrayfield with the boys. I want them to remember this day for the rest of their lives.

*I* certainly will. It's my last match; a dream. I've collected the best players from all over the world, put them down on my favourite rugby ground and now all I have to do is to make sure that the supporters enjoy the match . . . and that my side wins.

It's all in my imagination, but what a game it should be. Rugby players, whether they are puffing and panting members of the Extra Third XV or British Lions, are no different from the fans. They all have their own ideas about who are the all-time greats. And everyone has his own opinion.

At least I have had the advantage of playing with or against every single player who will run out on to Murrayfield this afternoon while the crowd roars and the Lion Rampant flags are waved. I've got the scars to prove it. But picking these two teams was not easy. Many friends made over the years have had to be content with a complimentary seat in the stand and an invitation to a party-after which should break every world record for celebration tonight.

The Rest of the World side have been arriving at Turnhouse Airport over the last two days. They are all present, correct and fit. I scan my eyes over the programme and think again about the tactics which will be necessary to contain them. It will not be easy. I go through the team!

Jean Michel Aguirre (France)

Grant Batty (New Zealand)
Roland Bertranne (France)
Bruce Robertson (New Zealand)
Stu Wilson (New Zealand)

Hugo Porto (Argentina)
John Hipwell (Australia)

Jean Iracabal (France)
Andy Dalton (New Zealand)
Hannes Marais (South Africa)
Colin Meads (New Zealand)
Andy Hayden (New Zealand)
Graham Mourie (New Zealand)
Benoit Dauga (France)
Jean Pierre Rives (France)

As the one-and-only selector, I can claim that at least the side wasn't a committee decision. It's my head on the chopping block and I know full well that I could have picked fifteen other players just as good as the people at this moment making their way down Haymarket and onto the ground. I had a few sleepless nights before I made the final decision with Eileen complaining about me pacing up and down the bedroom at three o' clock in the morning. Let's consider just what went through my mind as I faced the unenviable task of picking the best of the best.

At fullback, Jean Michel Aguire had to head off quite a few contenders before he won his place, chiefly from another Frenchman, Pierre Villepreux, and two All Blacks, Joe Karam and Fergie McCormack. In the end it came down to a straight fight between the two French, both of whom have tremendous flair which, combined with great speed, made them menacing in attack. They were both part of the French tradition of opening up play from the most unexpected places and turning unlikely situations into a springboard for an attack which might score a try 70 yards and half-a-dozen seconds later. I gave the nod, eventually, to Jean Michel because on top of that flair he had extra defensive qualities. One of the first attributes you look for in any fullback is his ability to field the high ball consistently under pressure. It takes bravery to do that with a modern mobile pack bearing down on you. The great fullback will take the ball even if half-a-dozen bulldozers are due to arrive a split second later. When he's got the ball safely, you want a fullback to kick it into touch all the time. A kick of length is a bit of a bonus. The first requirement is to put the ball out of play. I considered that Jean Michel did all those things better than any other man. And on top of that, when he tackled you, you stayed tackled.

On the wings, Bryan Williams, Jean Francois Gourdon and Jean Cantoni all forced their way into consideration but there was never much doubt in my mind whom I would ask to travel all across the world to play. New Zealanders Grant Batty and Stu Wilson are great crowd-pleasers, threequarters of very contrasting styles but men who have one quality in common which I must admire. Many wings are content to stay put and wait for others to bring them into the match, but not these two. They both want to be involved all the time and, if the situation allows it, they will both go looking for the ball.

In that way, they not only enjoy their rugby all the more, but they are more useful to a team.

Apart from that they are very different individuals. Grant sums up all those qualities which have always been important to the All Blacks. He has a total determination to win. Success is all-important to him. That, combined with constant alertness, makes him the kind of player you simply cannot afford to ignore for a single moment.

I'll always remember the try Grant scored for New Zealand against the Barbarians in 1972. He kicked the ball over the head of J.P.R. Williams – which is a much cleverer thing to do than invite a tackle from that particular gentleman – sprinted round him and went over. It demonstrated to me a desperation to score – and for a small man he's deceptively fast and strong.

Stu is a different kind of character altogether. He looks the part; slim and athletic. There's an image of All Black wingers as men who are content to stay deep, field the ball and then just hump it into touch – a kind of auxiliary fullback. But Stu put that myth firmly into touch with his opening run against Wales in 1979 to prove he wasn't afraid to launch attacks from some surprising places. Certainly both Stu and Grant have good enough football brains to drop deep and give Jean Michel help if the fullback needs it, but their games are far more highly developed than that.

The Rest of the World centres were hard to pick, simply because there seem to have been an endless stream of exceptional ones since I began my international rugby career. Jo Mazo, Jean Pierre Lux and Jean Trillo all come to mind. Ian McCrae of New Zealand, Joggie Jansen of South Africa and John Brass of Australia were others for whom I had a great deal of respect.

But no one really threatened Roland Bertranne because he is quite simply the best ball-handler that I have ever seen and rugby, after all, is a handling game. I can't honestly say that I ever remember him dropping a pass and that's an incredible achievement, bearing in mind the pressures of international matches. His hands were very quick and he could take a pass and give it almost in one movement. That quality meant it must have been a delight to play outside him because the half break was frequently made through that sleight of hand. And Roland, uncharacteristically for a Frenchman, couldn't be faulted as far as defensive play was concerned. He was a robust tackler, almost unpassable.

Bruce Robertson would be the perfect foil to Roland. Like Stu on the wing, he looks the part; strong, athletic, very fast and exceptionally good in defence. There's no point in picking a side which has two marvellous wingers and a fullback always prepared to come into the line if they are not going to see much of the ball, and Bruce is the man who would fit into that overall tactical plan.

My choice of Hugo Porto of Argentina at fly-half is unfashionable and will surprise many people. There were a lot of good men and true queuing up all over the world waiting for an invitation, but in the end I told Hugo to get on the transatlantic flight from Buenos Aires. Gerald Bosch of South Africa, Bob Burgess of New Zealand, Phil Hawthorne of Australia and Jean Pierre Romeu of France were all in the running.

But Hugo has the lot. I think one of the greatest skills in rugby is the way that a fly-half can drag the breakaway forwards to him, then glide past them, rather like a matador putting the bull exactly where he wants it. The secret is being well-balanced yourself and watching the forwards to see how they are balanced. Then – bingo – you make your move and float past them, leaving the guys either on the ground or clutching at thin air. That is the art of fly-half play but only part of a great one's repertoire. Hugo has a lot more going for him. He can kick well and with both feet – which is a bonus in tight defensive situations, particularly behind your own line. He can run as well. But above all, the fly-half is the main reader of the game, the nerve centre of operations, the link between the forwards and the backs. Whenever I played against Hugo I understood what he was trying to do for his side, summing up the overall situation and playing to Argentina's strengths. He's been the main influence on Argentinian rugby as it makes its way up towards complete parity with the major countries.

I've chosen John Hipwell of Australia as Hugo's partner at scrum-half, although this really was a position in which there wasn't much to choose between a whole clutch of players. If I had picked Dawie de Villiers, Dave Loveridge, Mark Donaldson or particularly Sid Going, I don't think it would have made a scrap of difference overall. Now I see why selectors have a hard – maybe impossible – choice. In the end you have to decide upon someone and for me it was the Aussie. He has two qualities which compliment each other. He's so strong that he can do his share round the base of the scrum, and is able to break through tackles and go himself. But his pass is also long enough to give the fly-half and centres that extra yard and that fraction of a second, to elude the cover. So John is an all-rounder in the best sense, and like all great scrum-halves, he doesn't take a breather during a match. He's a tireless worker in a difficult and very responsible position.

In the front row, the choice was between Hannes Marais and the Frenchman Jean Luis Azarete, André Vacquerin and Robert Paparemborde. In the end the South African won the vote – and that means I am going to have the hardest match of my life. Hannes, if you met him in the street, wouldn't impress you as a rugby man. But on the field he is something again, a strong scrummager and a good ball-handler who gets about the pitch alarmingly well. He could almost play front row and back row at the same time.

The challengers for the hooker's berth were Gies Pitzer of South Africa, the French pair of Paco and Benesis, and the New Zealander Ken Norton. But I gave it to Norton's All Black successor Andy Dalton. No matter what pressure you put on the props, Andy always seems to win the ball. He's a clever scrummager and a fine line-out thrower. He's mobile enough to set up tries as he did against Ireland in the 1977–78 tour.

To complete the front row, Moff Myburgh of South Africa was a contender but to give it complete international flavour I've gone for Jean Iracabal of France. Like me, he is strong, fast, a good scrummager and a fine support player!

In the second row, sheer physical bulk is an important factor. Size has to be supplemented by other plus-points and we can all think of locks who looked the part but didn't quite 'punch' their weight. But it's impossible to play in the position if you haven't got the height and weight needed both in the scrums and line-outs. There have been a lot of good big 'uns about in my time. Men like Frik Du Preez, Garrick Fay, Elie Cester, Peter Whiting – the list is considerable.

But who could oppose Colin 'Pinetree' Meads? For years he *was* rugby in New Zealand and that was an accolade bestowed upon the man as much as the player. He summed up All Blacks rugby: hard, mean, determined and committed. A wonderful person. And not only did he walk into this Rest of the World side, but he was the only possible choice of captain. Even among the giants of the game, he stands tall.

To partner him I chose another All Black to keep him company: Andy Hayden. But Andy had to resist a strong challenge from Du Preez. On top of his skill as a line-out jumper and his scrummaging power, Andy got about the field surprisingly quickly for a big man and was among the first to any maul.

I had to think a long time before picking the Number Eight. There were Jean Pierre Bastiat and Walter Spanghero of France, Alex Wylie and Andy Leslie of New Zealand, Mornie du Plessis and Tommy Bedford of South Africa, and Mark Loane of Australia. For a long time, I had Alex Wylie in the side because my mind went back to the British Lion's Third Test in New Zealand in 1971. We were winning the match comfortably and taking the lead in the series. The All Blacks, with Brian Lohore brought back, were in severe trouble up front and when Barry John scored those early points, there were a few New Zealand heads going down. Not Alex's though. He played his heart out in a lost cause and my respect for him – already great – grew the longer the game lasted. Here was one man who wouldn't quit. That makes him the sort of guy you want on your side.

But eventually it had to be the Frenchman Benoit Dauga. When Benoit has the ball in his hand, it looks like an orange. He's big, so he dominates the back of any line-out. And his support play and cover tackling just won him the place. But just thinking of Alex in the stand as a replacement makes me shudder at the depth of talent available to this Rest of the World side.

There was almost a busload of wing forwards to chose from. The All Backs, for example, throw them up as if they were coming off a conveyor belt – Ian Kirkpatrick, Ken Stewart, Lester Routledge. Piet Grayling and Jan Ellis of South Africa also come out of the top drawer. So does Greg Davis of Australia.

But just as I chose one New Zealand captain unopposed for one of the locks, so I picked another here. Graham Mourie is a lesson to any youngster learning the game. Graham realizes that before he does anything else he must take his share of the menial tasks, seeking the ball and tidying up. Only after that has been accomplished can he afford to begin the more glamorous stuff. And he's good at that. Graham is creative and intelligent. I try to count the number of times that one of his passes led to an All Black try and I give up. Times without number.

As a contrast, I picked Jean Pierre Rives, the action man. I had a little laugh over what would be a personal battle between Jean Pierre and Graham to see who could cover every inch of Murrayfield first. By the end of this match, both of them will have touched every blade of grass on the pitch about half-a-dozen times. They call Jean Pierre the blond bombshell and that's exactly what he is.

So I rang up the fifteen players and told them to get over here for the game. But I added a warning. Don't think it will be easy, and concluded for good measure with the statement that good as they might be, they were in for a drubbing. Because I've no doubt at all in my mind that this Rest of the World side has now met its match: that the Great Britain and Ireland team would beat them into the ground.

Well, they have arrived and in a few hours' time they are going to have to take their medicine. Because looking around at the old familiar faces of a squad just itching to get on the coach and motor into Murrayfield, I know that I am surrounded by the best men ever to have played the game.

Picking the Great Britain and Ireland team was even harder, apart from one place. The loose head prop is Ian

McLauchlan (Jordanhill and Scotland). It so happens, not being a character noted for his mock modesty, that I deserve a place as of right. But in any case, it's my match and as sole selector of this squad as well, there's nothing much anyone can do about it. I look down our teamsheet:

J.P.R. Williams (Wales)

Gerald Davies (Wales)
Mike Gibson (Ireland)
Jim Renwick (Scotland)
David Duckham (England)

Barry John (Wales)
Gareth Edwards (Wales)

Ian McLauchlan (Scotland)
Bobby Windsor (Wales)
Graham Price (Wales)
Willie John McBride (Ireland)
Gordon Brown (Scotland)
Fergus Slattery (Ireland)
Mervyn Davies (Wales)
Tony Nearey (England)

Bob Hiller, Andy Irvine and Tom Kiernan were all possible choices for full-back. Hiller could kick, Andy could kick and run, whilst Tom was as good a sound, all-round full-back as any. But how do you compare mere mortals with the Rock of Gibraltar, which was the nickname we gave to J.P.R. Williams. I once asked J.P.R. how he coped at full-back when he was the only player standing between two opposing three-quarters and his own line. 'Imagine,' I said, 'you are on your own, there's no cover behind you and the two coming at you are class players, full of speed.'

'Well,' he replied, 'You'd have to fancy that they would score. At least one of them would score but the other would be carried off.' That tells you all you need to know about J.P.R.'s defensive qualities and the way he stands under the high kick and fields it, every time, with a herd of buffaloes arriving simultaneously is part of the legend of rugby. As a runner he was fearless too. His breaks up the middle were so fast and aggressive that it was remarkable the number of times he went all the way, even against the best class of opposition. But if he was grounded, he was grounded in the right place with the forwards able to arrive quickly to get possession and start up another attack. With J.P.R. behind us, it will be like playing with a brick wall facing the Rest of the World.

On the wings I have chosen one Englishman and one Welshman. Billy Steele and Bill Gammell of Scotland, Tom Grace and Dixie Duggan of Ireland were all on the short list – but as with J.P.R. the final choice didn't take a lot of heart-searching. Like Grant Batty and Stu Wilson in the Rest of the World team, I think that it is important to pick two men of contrasting styles – so I have come up with David Duckham and Gerald Davies. They are both dangerous but they are both very different.

David is a well-balanced runner, a creative wing able to do his share of defending. He's a natural sportsman who understands instinctively what is on and what's not. He's a determined runner when he has the line in his sight. Gerald is very different: a right little twinkletoes. I suppose that compared to the flying machines which have been part of rugby down the years, Gerald hasn't got that all-out devastating pace. But maybe he never needed it. His ability was always best seen in tight situations. You would look across the field and see him hemmed in by half-a-dozen defenders and with very little room to play with. Then suddenly, they were all looking round and wondering which way he had gone. The secret was in the sidesteps and the dummying. He could jink past almost anyone – a case of now you see him, now you don't.

One of my choices for the centre will cause absolutely no controversy and the other will lead to a lot of argument. The selection of Mike Gibson, with his record number of Irish caps, speaks for itself and he must be in the side as another natural sportsman and all-round rugby player. He gains preference over John Spencer, Geoff Evans, Arthur Lewis, Steve Fenwick, Roy Bergier and a host of others. But the other choice leaves me open to allegations relating to the Old Pals Act.

But I have no hesitation in picking Hawick's Jim Renwick to partner Gibson. For almost ten years now Jim has been in a class of his own and how he was never taken on the 1977 British Lions tour of New Zealand is a constant source of amazement to me. At least, I'm not going to make the same mistake John Dawes and the selectors made on that occasion. I have to declare an interest and say that he's one of the best guys I've ever met, but that's not the reason why he's in the side. He has every technical ability you need and he's got a very sharp rugby brain as well. Alongside Gibson he could be a revelation – as the top brass finally admitted when they picked him for the Lions tour of South Africa this year.

There are no prizes for guessing the half-back pairing. Barry John and Gareth Edwards, the great heroes of Welsh rugby, are my heroes as well. Barry is 'The King' and that says it all: the complete player who has all the qualities that Hugo Porta will show on the other side and that incalculable extra commodity. In a word he's a genius. Curiously though, if Barry were unavailable I would have no hesitation in picking Alan Old, which again puts me at odds with the Establishment selectors. England have never appreciated him as much as they should have done. But even Alan would have to admit that with Barry around, there's not much of a contest.

Gareth, quite simply, is the best rugby player there has ever been. From my position in the team, I can name his number one asset – he always puts the ball where the forwards want it. Playing for the Lions it was quite astonishing how often we would win the scrummage and, hardly looking up, just trot thirty or forty yards up to the line-out. We knew Gareth would put the ball there every time. Then we would win the line-out and go forward another thirty yards, thanks to the next kick. When Gareth was asked to be photographed for a coaching manual, the experts looked at the pictures, noted where his feet were and concluded that he did it all wrong. That's another hallmark of his genius. That he does it his own way. I'd have Dougie Morgan, that marvellous enthusiast, sitting on the bench in case anything happened to Gareth. But I doubt if it would.

The Great Britain and Ireland front row would comprise McLauchlan, Bobby Windsor and Graham Price. Bobby, as you probably realize by now, is another good buddy but, like Jim Renwick, he gets into the team on merit alone. Bobby loves scrummaging. He couldn't wait to get up from one scrum to be involved in the next. Of course, there have been other fine hookers over this period – notably John Pullin, Ken Kennedy, Duncan Madsen and Colin Fisher – but Bobby wins the day because he is that bit quicker around the field. And as a line-out thrower he was among the best at catching people napping and throwing the ball where it could cause maximum damage.

You would have to put Graham on the other side because of his experience and ability. But not just that. The front row is where you have to be absolutely certain that the others are on your side. I'd much rather have him playing with me than against me. To complete the front five of this all-time Mean Machine, I had to pick Willie John McBride because he has become a legend in his own playing lifetime. Like J.P.R., Barry and Gareth, he was an automatic choice. Picking the other lock was more difficult.

Based on home performances, I would have picked the England and British Lions captain Billy Beaumont because he is probably the most consistent lock in all four countries. Delme Thomas, Moss Kean, Alistair McHarg and Brian Price would do more than a fair turn for any side. But eventually I settled on Gordon Brown. 'Babyface Broon' may look like an angel. Meet him in the street and you wouldn't think he could harm a flea. In club matches he can sometimes take that docile attitude onto the pitch. But put him in a Scotland or British Lions jersey and the nice guy turns into a tiger. On a personal note, he is the best scrummager I have ever had behind me.

For the Number Eight slot there were a few contenders – Peter Dixon, Roger Uttley, Andy Ripley, Willie Duggan and Jim Telfer. But once more it didn't take me long to find the natural and obvious choice. 'Merve the Swerve' Davies is a remarkable man physically. He comes in at about six foot six inches and with arms that seem to stretch down to his knees.

That kind of physique – a sort of telescopic man – made him just about unbeatable at the tail of the line-out, but Merve's contribution didn't end there. He could get all over the field and many a time I've looked at him and said to myself, 'You've no right to be there.' But somehow Merve had made it.

The most difficult personal decision came at wing forward. I dearly wanted to find a place for another friend, Nairn McEwan. I wanted to do so to right the same injustice done to Jim Renwick in 1977. He was another who didn't go on tour when he had every right to do so. But in the end I had to go for Fergus Slattery and Tony Nearey, although still with some hesitation because there wasn't a cigarette paper's bit of difference between their skills and those of Nairn. Slatts, though, was so fast that he could put endless pressure on the fly-half and centres, while having a fierce commitment to the ball himself. Tony, both in defence and attack, is the best flanker for many a day in the four home countries.

By now, the cold chicken and chablis has been devoured in the Murrayfield car parks, the hampers are being put away and the stand is as full as the terraces. In the dressing rooms, the feet are clattering on the floor but there is still time for me to go and have a word with the referee and wish him a good match. It doesn't do any harm to try and get him on your side. Not that I have much chance with this man.

A good referee can make a match. A bad one can ruin it. I had no second thoughts about the man I wanted – that splendid Borderer Bob Burrell. There are so many stories about Bob and most of them are true. There was the time he was walking along a dressing room corridor and heard the home team captain giving his pre-match pep-talk, concluding with the words: 'And watch out for this referee, he's an absolute bastard'. Bob said nothing then, but as soon as the home side kicked off he awarded a penalty. 'What was that for?' asked the captain. 'For impugning my Mother before the match,' he said.

There was another occasion when even Bob was having trouble with a couple of front rows who weren't exactly seeing eye to eye. And that's putting it mildly. Bob broke up the scrum yet again and was beginning to lose patience: 'Look,' he said: 'I've just had an idea. If you don't cut it out, I'll make the front rows play in the back row and the back rows play in the front row.' The thought of flankers having to hook and props having to run about all over the pitch at the double soon sorted all that out. That was the kind of referee Bob was. He commanded complete respect and gained total authority. But all he said was laced with a marvellous sense of humour. And stories about him, told in Gala slang, would certainly be the high point of the after-match dinner.

The match kicks off and an hour-and-a-half later I am carried back into the dressing room shoulder-high. A last-minute try by McLauchlan has given the Great Britain and Ireland team a 41–40 victory over the Rest of the World. I'll leave Norman Mair to give you the rest of the details in the *Scotsman*. And the selectors arrive to tell me that I am not only to be captain of the first World XV, but seeing as I am so clever, I can pick the side myself and take it off on tour for three months. Eileen and the boys will be highly delighted. I choose the following team:

J.P.R. Williams (Wales)

Gerald Davies (Wales)
Roland Bertranne (France)
Jim Renwick (Scotland)
Stu Wilson (New Zealand)

Barry John (Wales)
Gareth Edwards (Wales)

Ian McLauchlan (Scotland)
Bobby Windsor (Wales)
Graham Price (Wales)
Colin Meads (New Zealand)
Willie John McBride (Ireland)
Graham Mourie (New Zealand)
Mervyn Davies (Wales)
Jean Pierre Rives (France)

We are going on tour. Pack the bags.

# 15

# End Game

The other holidaymakers at La Turballe, Brittany, must have thought that I was mad. Eileen and the boys were used to it by now. At the end of a day on the beach I would head towards the local football ground and start training. While most of the other people on the camping site were sitting around outside the tents, sipping their pre-dinner drinks, this track-suited figure, coated in sweat, was grunting and groaning his way towards fitness.

It was Summer 1979. By now I was officially tagged a veteran. I was getting used to pimply-faced opponents coming up to me during a match and saying: 'My Dad played against you.' But a last prize was waiting in my career – a chance to play against the All Blacks again and try to help gain the first Scottish win over them since the series started back in 1905. I was determined to have a go.

I felt good that summer. To be honest, I had expected my international career to come to an end the previous season because I couldn't shake off a whole series of niggling injuries. I would wake up some Monday mornings after a Saturday match and then a Sunday squad session with the International pool at Murrayfield and feel hellish. My performance on the field wasn't suffering but the knocks were becoming harder to get over. But I wanted a last crack at it.

If I were to get into the Scottish team, I knew I had to be fit. Hence the daily training stints on holiday. People often ask what the prime requirements of a loose head prop are and I try to answer, without going into the technical aspects of the game, the ways in which you can manipulate your opponents in the scrum and the ways in which you can legally block in the line-out. To me, the most important factor is that a front five forward needs to be able to run and run – and then run some more.

Throughout my career, training has been based on that belief. If you can run and get around the field and still feel strong in the closing part of a game when most other people's legs are beginning to melt, then the chances are that you will receive some recognition in the game. There's hardly been a day in the last twenty years when I wasn't out running and the sight of McLauchlan in his track-suit in the Corstorphine area of Edinburgh where I live has become about as common as the milkman or postman out on their rounds.

At the start of every season I planned out a schedule which included a daily couple of miles. Once that initial stamina work had been done, I would cut it down and concentrate on speed training until I was not just strong but pretty quick about the pitch. The schedules were originally worked out by Bill Dickinson and haven't varied much over the years. Topped up with weight-training it all combined to produce physical hardness, as much speed as possible, and strength.

I say hardness because, as you will already have realized, that is what is required. A prop – or any front five man – has to be able to get about, knock guys down, get knocked down himself and keep on making the tackles. What happens in the tight and the line-out may be the basis of your value to the team, but if you can add mobility then it's obvious you can make a far greater contribution to overall team play.

All this was going through my mind in France. Life may not begin at thirty-seven but I didn't see any reason why my career should come to a stop. Not just yet. It wasn't easy in the heat of the summer but knowing that my age was going to be something of a disadvantage in the selector's minds at least, it was important to impress them early on. I was prepared to make that effort of will.

Every night I ran round the football pitch eight times, which represented two miles, and I was timing myself trying to get inside twelve minutes. That may not win any gold medals at an Olympics but it was a fairly realistic target to set. I would follow that up with ten lengths of the field, timed again and with a recovery-period of thirty seconds. Then I would finish off with a series of press-ups and sit-ups. Eileen would then greet her husband, stinking with sweat. But after a shower and an evening meal, I was feeling really good.

We came home early to be ready for the first National Squad session at Jordanhill. To an extent, although I'd done all this running, it is irrelevant to what actually happens on the field. I remember Willie John McBride saying to the Lions: 'You might be able to beat me in any training session but you just try and outrun me in an actual game.' The Scottish international Ian Barnes was another man who was a different person in the heat of battle. If you kicked the ball forty yards forward during a match, 'Barney' would always be among the first five out of sixteen forwards to arrive. He knew all the short cuts on a pitch and how to use them. The point is that fitness is essential – but there's a lot more to it than that.

That first squad session went well and there was an unexpected bonus in this bid to prove myself. I had been invited to Boston to coach the local rugby side there and for two weeks I had plenty of exercise. I coached Monday, Tuesday, Thursday, Friday, Saturday and Sunday of both weeks and if I wasn't putting others through their paces, I was training myself.

I got caught up in the American jogging cult and was out most evenings covering five miles, chatting away to my companions all the time and discovering what a pride they took in physical fitness. The weather in Boston was very, very warm and I came back feeling I was as near to top shape as I ever had been.

For Jordanhill, the season started poorly. It ended up with relegation from the First Division and that cast some gloom over my last season. The standard wasn't high but we couldn't seem to get going. But as far as the International scene was concerned, I was building up to a peak all the time.

November came round and the All Blacks match loomed. Two days before the team was announced, I heard a whisper that the selectors were considering me for the captaincy – the greatest honour in the game. I was astonished; I thought it was a joke. But when the side was announced, I was skipper for the first time since 1976. All the hard work had paid off.

It was a cool clear day at Murrayfield. When we woke up, had breakfast in the Braidhills and settled down to read the papers, there seemed to be an air of confidence amongst the Rugby writers. I shared their optimism because this was not the greatest All Blacks side to come to this country, despite the marvellous leadership of Graham Mourie and the running skills of Stu Wilson. We had thought long and hard about the way to tackle the match and come to the conclusion that if we took the game to them it could lead to Scotland breaking that duck.

In the end it was a disaster. The forwards played particularly well and the backs played particularly badly. You'll never win any game if you commit the number of basic elementary mistakes that Scotland did on that depressing afternoon. To take the game to the All Blacks was a considerable challenge but the guys simply didn't respond to it.

The catalogue of errors was substantial. We dropped the ball when we had it, we failed to find touch when we needed it and the whole thing was a cock-up. To make matters worse, we were doing all the groundwork which should have given us the platform for a win. The All Blacks were beaten in the scrums and they were beaten in the line-outs – but still we never managed to play the game in their pressure zone. We were forced back by our own stupidity.

The All Blacks had only limited possession but, all credit to them, they made the most of it. They scored four tries, the most depressing one coming when Murray Mexted waltzed through and over from a line-out. Dave Loveridge, Stu Wilson and Richard Wilson scored the others and all we had to show for it were two Andy Irvine penalties. In the end it was 20–6, the flags had been pulled down and if the 60,000 crowd which left Murrayfield was disappointed, I couldn't blame them.

I felt sorry for a lot of people. There was Tom Pearson, the chairman of selectors who had made a conscious – and successful – effort to get on the same wavelength as the players and who was as dejected as the rest of us. Nairn McEwan felt terrible about it. At the press conference, I managed to mutter a few words of praise for the All Blacks and congratulate my own side for sticking to the task. But I suspect my face told the real story. It was a disaster.

It never dawned on me for a minute that following this match I would be dropped. No-one is more self-critical of his performance than myself and, sitting down later and analysing the game, I thought that I had been among the best of the forwards on either side.

The District season which followed was again a disaster. The squad sessions seemed endless and when the matches came round the bad weather forced postponements and switches of venues. It wasn't a happy time for Glasgow but my own form was holding up well.

Then disquieting rumours began to start. I found out through the back door that my selection for the All Blacks game had terms and conditions placed upon it. Tom Pearson had been told to inform me that I was there to do a job for Scotland, but if I didn't do it, then the selectors would find it hard to keep me in the side. In effect, they had laid the captaincy on me because they didn't have anyone else in mind for the post.

But Tom had never told me that it might be curtains. He'd simply said that I was captain and to crack on with the job. Then he went down with a heart attack and his presence was removed from the committee.

So at the start of the Five Nations Championship, I wasn't in the team for the match against Ireland. To put it mildly, I was very, very upset. There had been a lot of pressure – understandably – in the press for changes after the New Zealand game and the picture had been further confused by the Scotland 'B' team winning two matches, against Ireland and France. I took those wins as creditable but thought the results should be treated with some caution. The French, after all, had played a side which showed thirteen changes from the team which had earlier beaten England.

What really annoyed me was that my place had been gained by Jim Burnett, who had been playing in the 'B' squad. Jim is thirty-two. I wouldn't have minded so much if my successor had been a man in his twenties who had a few

years of rugby in front of him. But that selection seemed to be·
a step backwards, as subsequent internationals proved.

I was told (on the telephone) that I was dropped when
another of the selectors, Robin Charters of Hawick, rang me
at home. He informed me that Burnett would be in. I said that
I wasn't happy and asked him if he would be good enough to
give some reasons. He mentioned the successes of the 'B' team
and generally hummed and hawed. But he simply wouldn't
tell me if the real reason was that I was too old, or that I was
too slow, or the selectors thought that my scrummaging
wasn't good enough. He did say that he would speak to me at
the next squad session. 'Don't bet on me being there,' I
replied angrily and hung up.

When the side to meet Ireland was officially announced I
was even more upset. The selectors had dropped half the
pack – the forwards were being made to take the blame and
they had been the best part of the side against the New
Zealanders. And to make matters worse, three of those dropped – Gordon Dickson, the wing forward, scrum-half Alan
Lawson and winger Keith Robertson – were all included as
replacements. Now it's general practice when naming a
reserve for the props to nominate the loose head man because
that is where the ball is won and lost. It's a bit easier playing
tight head. But McLauchlan's name didn't come into it at
all.

I got over the anger I had shown on the phone and decided
that I would go to the squad session. I thought that as I had
seen it through this far I might as well go the whole hog. But I
sought out Charters and asked why I wasn't even considered
as a replacement.

'We've appointed a new captain as you know – Mike
Biggar. And we thought that it would be better for him to
have a fresh start without the former skipper being in the
side.' That really made me see red, because anyone who
knows about Mike and myself would understand that he
would never do anything to prejudice my chances as captain
and I would never do anything to prejudice his. It just showed
how little selectors know about players.

Another selector sought me out that day: Ian McGregor,

who had taken over from Tom Pearson as the acting chairman. 'I know how you feel,' he said. 'You have no conception at all how I feel,' I replied. 'Suit yourself,' he added, and walked away. That was the last time I spoke to him.

The season was turning into a nightmare. I had half resolved to quit after the All Blacks match and was rather wishing that I had done so. The reason was that there had been another incident which cast a pall of gloom over me. This was all the publicity stirred up after a League game between Jordanhill and Kelso. It concerned Eric Paxton.

It all started during just another ruck in just another match. The ruck broke up and the ball was kicked into touch and no-one thought any more about it. But the Kelso man left the field with a bad gash in his head, was taken off to hospital and eventually had to have stitches put into the wound. That, as far as we were all concerned, was that: a regrettable injury but one of those accidents which have happened before those and will happen again. The game went on as before. The Kelso players didn't think anything untoward had happened. Knowing a fair few of them quite well, I am sure that, had they thought that a teammate had been deliberately injured, they would not only have remarked upon it, but their reaction would have been one of extreme violence. I wouldn't have blamed them because deliberate kicking is completely out of order. The point was that it didn't happen like that.

Paxton didn't go off to hospital straight away. He watched the rest of the match from the touchline, then visited the Western Infirmary, had the wound patched up and still managed to come back to the clubhouse and have a drink with us before the Kelso team left for home in the Borders.

I want to state quite categorically that the incident was not intentional. Jordanhill held a full inquiry. The committee invited anyone to come to a meeting who might have been able to shed any light on the incident, not just players but also spectators. No one had seen anything untoward: no one could throw any light on it. I have played a long time with Jordanhill and know most of the players in the team: none of them has ever shown any psychopathic tendencies. We just do not deliberately kick anyone on the ground.

That should have been an end to it, but in the papers the following week, Margaret Thatcher, President Carter and the Shah of Iran all got short measure because of the beanfeast made over the incident. The adverse publicity to which the Kelso club subjected my club in the days that followed did nothing for the image of rugby, the good of the game in general, or Jordanhill in particular. Kelso discredited themselves by not dealing with the matter privately. Instead they washed their dirty linen in public. And in letters to Jordanhill, they named two players and said that they thought one of them might have been involved. Then they mentioned the names of two *other* players and said that one of them might have been involved. So that covered half the scrum – blanket coverage. It was all absurd.

I don't blame the papers for latching on to the story. They didn't have far to look with Kelso putting out all these statements. But I don't think that's the way clubs should conduct themselves. Looking back, it was a storm in a teacup but it was the kind of aggravation I could have done without at this stage of my career.

I wasn't happy, either, with the way the strains and stresses of modern international rugby were getting to my friend Nairn McEwan, the national coach and member of the selection committee. He was still seeking his first win since taking on the job over two years before, and was looking to stop a rout of twelve games without a win. Over the last months I had seen a great change in him as a coach and in his relationship with the players. Nairn's contribution as coach had been immense and the cost to him, with the constant travel from Inverness to Edinburgh, considerable. But throughout the last season I thought that he was not getting the players he wanted for the kind of rugby he espoused. He wanted a fifteen-man game but he knew that the basis of that kind of play is regular and good possession of the ball.

Part of the problem is that the SRU hasn't adopted the

sensible way of doing things and made the coach Chairman of the Selectors as well. After all, he knows the players more intimately, he is clear on the type of tactics he will use and, most important of all, it's his head which goes on the chopping block when things go wrong. He should at least have the casting vote on selection. Indeed I would like to see a situation where *he* named the team, with the other selectors acting as a safety valve in case the coach did anything really outrageous. Nairn was used by the SRU – but never given their full support.

I watched the Scotland game against Ireland in Dublin on TV and looked on in frustration. For a while it looked as if Nairn would be rewarded with some success at last and for a few minutes my hopes rose. It's one thing to be acutely disappointed at not being picked; it's quite another not to wish them well. I had sent them a goodluck telegram before the match and was cheering them on like everyone else as Andy kicked us into a lead and then John Rutherford sliced his way through to present David Johnston with his first try in international rugby. I could see, even on television, what went wrong later. The scrummage wasn't right, there was no blocking in the line-out and when the Irish found their feet they were too fast and furious for the Scots. They scored the next 22 points in the game and by the time David Johnston scored his second try and Andy converted, it was far too late. There just wasn't enough craft in the side and I was angry about that.

I thought I would be back against France – but I wasn't. Instead I was a paying member of the public in the centre stand at Murrayfield. Thank goodness the spectators round about me must have understood how I felt because they kept very quiet and Eileen didn't say much either. She knew the mood I was in, and knows I like to watch my rugby in silence anyway.

Scotland won and I was pleased at that. But it was a bit of a fluke. France got so much of the ball, but they wasted it and then Andy, who had been digging his own grave at the start of the game, hit one of those magical patches. He scored 16 points in the last fourteen minutes: part of the finest fight-back that even he – who seems to step right out of the pages of *Boys Own* – could contrive. That carried the crowd into ecstasy and they forgot and forgave his six muffed penalties earlier on. I can't say I blame them and at last Nairn had got the win he had worked so hard for. Andy's mesmeric running may have won the game for us, but I'll never forget the real turning point, when John Beattie got the ball and went forward: it took four Frenchmen to pull him down. Suddenly confidence surged through the side. I'll bet John never forgets it either, because it was at that moment he served notice that there was no way he could be left out of the British Lions squad for the tour of South Africa. 'If *he* can do it, if a young and inexperienced player can do it, so can the rest of us.' I almost heard the lads saying that to themselves.

I continued to go to the squad sessions and suddenly found myself back on the bench as a replacement for the match against Wales in Cardiff. That was a strange game. Wales had just played England in the Battle of Waterloo at Twickenham in which Paul Ringer had been sent off. Obviously they were under orders to play a low-key game and they did so. They didn't need to do much more, as Scotland didn't have any answers for them. They scored at will and were content to run up 17 points before Jim Renwick scored in the final seconds and Andy converted. It was an afternoon tinged with sadness for me. I felt the frustration of seeing things go wrong – at one stage Graham Price ran all the way through our line-out to tackle fly-half Brian Gossman, something which should be impossible at this level. But the Cardiff crowd didn't revel in the win: there was hardly any singing and it was sad to leave that ground for the last time without hearing the fervour of the world's most patriotic supporters. Even in defeat, that would have been a memory to take home for ever.

That left England, who were chasing the Grand Slam. I knew a week before that I wasn't going to be in the side because no selector came to watch Jordanhill's match with Watsonians. I'd maybe grasped at straws because I thought that Scotland would definitely need me for the battle with

England's Power Pack. But the selectors thought that the team in Wales had done frightfully well and in their infinite wisdom all they did was drop the captain Mike Biggar. As it turned out Mike came back after Gordon Dickson caught flu – but Andy stayed captain and the selectors had broken a world record, picking three skippers in one season with no injuries forcing their hand. That – more than anything they did to me – showed just how worthy or otherwise they were of holding their jobs.

To sit on the bench was a humiliating experience. Perhaps it was because I had played so often for Scotland; I knew only too well the privilege of playing in the side and I didn't feel a member of the team at all. I was on the outside; there only because the selectors couldn't find anybody else.

I thought we were going back to the Dark Ages, returning to the bad old days when I first came into the Scottish team. Then, the selectors felt they were somewhere *up there* and the players somewhere *down there*. There was no communication between those who picked the men and the men themselves.

It all came home to me the day before the match at the Braidhills. The SRU, in its wisdom, had decided that the *à la carte* menu was off for the players. That didn't make much difference to the standard of the food, which is always good. But it was indicative of an attitude. Treat players like children and maybe they will react like children. It was like being told to eat the school dinner.

I was still fuming that none of them had had the guts to face me man to man, and explain why I wasn't wanted any more. If just one of them had found the courage to say that I was too old or not good enough any more, I would have accepted that and respected the man who said it. Selectors have that prerogative and over the years I have not been unused to harsh criticism. But all that happened was one long silence.

I just wanted to go out of the game feeling that there was still a place for me in it. If a selector had said to me, 'If you want to stay in the team, you will need to improve such-and-such an aspect of your game,' I would have accepted it and possibly replied that at my age I couldn't. Eileen says they're scared of me. But there's no reason for that. I'd have listened.

So I sat fully stripped, but with really nowhere to go, as England duly completed the Grand Slam in a match where Scotland's second-half revival, on top of England's first-half tries, made it a treat for the crowd. But we never had a hope of winning it.

I went to the dance that night. It was only fair on Eileen, who had sacrificed so much over the years. I even danced with her and that's unusual. I knew so much would never happen again.

The long lie-in on the morning of the game, the perusal of the newspapers, the coach trip across Edinburgh to Murrayfield, the hum of the crowd above the dressing room, the smell of wintergreen, the sight of the flags flying as we came out of the tunnel. The joy of coming back to the dressing room, a job well done, another cap well earned. The dejection of defeat. The jokes, the laughter, the cracks. I was for going home early to bed when I looked across the room and saw Johnny Beattie and Alan Tomes laughing.

They would soon be picked to go on tour with the British Lions. So too would Jim Renwick and that was better late than never. They would beat England one day. Maybe they would go to Wales and douse those choirs. That had been me.

I had got over the worst of it. The sadness and, I suppose, bitterness of the last season evaporated as I remembered the years that had gone before. Not so much the places; more the people. The famous ones who became friends and for whom my door will always be open. And the thousands met along the way joined by the brotherhood of rugby, who only wanted an autograph, who would have been mortally offended if I had not gone home with them and just given them my company.

I looked at Eileen and remembered how I had gone off to New Zealand and South Africa without too much regret because I was going to play rugby – and rugby was my game. I thought of Andrew, Scott and Ross, whose Dad sometimes wasn't there.

Tackle, tackle, tackle, knock them down, knock them down, knock them down. That had been a way of life for twenty years and maybe that was long enough. I was going home and leaving it to a new generation, who will find out the delights of a great game played with great characters.

Finished with rugby at thirty-seven, I was still considerably ahead of the game. We made our excuses and left.

# Career Record

## Scotland v. England

1969 Twickenham  Lost 8–3
1971 Twickenham  Won 16–15
1971 Murrayfield  Won 26–6 (Centenary International)
1972 Murrayfield  Won 23–9
1973 Twickenham  Lost 20–13*
1974 Murrayfield  Won 16–14*
1975 Twickenham  Lost 7–6
1976 Murrayfield  Won 22–12*
1978 Murrayfield  Lost 15–0*
1979 Twickenham  Drew 7–7


## Scotland v. Wales

1970 Cardiff       Lost 18–9
1971 Murrayfield  Lost 19–18
1972 Cardiff       Lost 35–12
1973 Murrayfield  Won 10–9*
1974 Cardiff       Lost 6–0*
1975 Murrayfield  Won 12–10
1976 Cardiff       Lost 28–6
1977 Murrayfield  Lost 18–9*
1978 Cardiff       Lost 22–14*
1979 Murrayfield  Lost 19–13

## Scotland v. Ireland

1971 Murrayfield Lost 15–0
1973 Murrayfield Won 19–14
1974 Dublin        Lost 9–6*
1975 Murrayfield Won 20–13
1976 Dublin        Won 15–6*
1978 Dublin        Lost 12–9*
1979 Murrayfield Drew 11–11


## Scotland v. France

1970 Murrayfield Lost 11–9
1971 Paris         Lost 13–8
1972 Murrayfield Won 20–9
1973 Paris         Lost 16–13
1974 Murrayfield Won 19–6*
1975 Paris         Lost 10–9
1976 Murrayfield Lost 13–6*
1978 Murrayfield Lost 19–16*
1979 Paris         Lost 21–17


## Scotland v. Other Countries

| 1969 | v. South Africa | Murrayfield | Won 6–3 |
| 1972 | v. New Zealand | Murrayfield | Lost 14–9* |
| 1973 | v. President's Overseas XV | Murrayfield | Won 27–16* |
| 1975 | v. New Zealand | Auckland | Lost 24–0* |
| 1975 | v. Australia | Sydney | Lost 23–3* |
| 1978 | v. New Zealand | Murrayfield | Lost 18–9* |
| 1979–80 | v. New Zealand | Murrayfield | Lost 20–6* |


43 caps, 19 times captain(*)

## British Lions

1971 *v.* New Zealand Dunedin     Won 9–3
1971 *v.* New Zealand Christchurch     Lost 22–12
1971 *v.* New Zealand Wellington     Won 13–3
1971 *v.* New Zealand Auckland     Drew 14–14
1974 *v.* South Africa Capetown     Won 12–3
1974 *v.* South Africa Pretoria     Won 28–9
1974 *v.* South Africa Port Elizabeth   Won 26–9
1974 *v.* South Africa Johannesburg   Drew 13–13


## Scotland Tours

1968–69 Argentina
1969–70 Australia
1975–76 New Zealand
1977–78 Japan and Far East


## Other games

1970 Barbarians *v.* Cardiff
1970 Barbarians *v.* Newport
1975 Barbarians *v.* New Zealand
1978 Barbarians *v.* North Midlands (captain)
1974 Irish Wolfhounds *v.* Gloucester
1974 Irish Wolfhounds *v.* Ebbw Vale
1974 Captain of Centenary Tour of International Wolfhounds
to Ireland